International Study Guide 35

A GUIDE TO DOING THEOLOGY

The International Study Guides

The global nature of Christianity has become perhaps its most defining feature in the last century. The need for resources that reflect this nature not only in topic but in approach and authorship has never been greater. To meet this need Fortress Press is proud to present a curated selection of volumes from the International Study Guides series. The product of a decades-long commitment on the part of the Society for Promoting Christian Knowledge (SPCK), the International Study Guides present projects in Bible, theology, and Christian history from a decidedly global vantage point.

International Study Guide

A Guide to Doing Theology
John Parratt

A GUIDE TO DOING THEOLOGY

Fortress Press Edition © 2015

Copyright © John Parratt 1996. All rights reserved. Except for brief quotations in critical articles or reviews, no part of this book may be reproduced in any manner without prior written permission from the publisher. Visit http://www.augsburgfortress.org/copyrights/ or write to Permissions, Augsburg Fortress, Box 1209, Minneapolis, MN 55440.

Unless otherwise noted, Scripture quotations are taken from the Revised Standard Version of the Bible, Ecumenical Edition, copyright © 1973 by the Division of Christian Education of the National Council of the Churches of Christ in the USA.

Cover design: Laurie Ingram

Library of Congress Cataloging-in-Publication Data
Print ISBN: 978-1-4514-9961-2
eBook ISBN: 978-1-5064-0027-3

The paper used in this publication meets the minimum requirements of American National Standard for Information Sciences — Permanence of Paper for Printed Library Materials, ANSI Z329.48-1984.

Manufactured in the U.S.

To Saroj Nalini

Preface

I am most grateful to Nicholas Beddow, former Editor of the SPCK International Study Guides, for initially suggesting that there is a need for a short introduction to theology, designed to stimulate original thinking and written from the non-Western context, and for his continued encouragement of this project. I am also most grateful to Daphne Terry for her editorial work on this volume.

I have approached this task with a number of basic assumptions in mind. First, that theology is not simply something that we learn about but, in the last analysis, is something which we *do* (hence the title of this Guide). Secondly, the way we do theology is profoundly influenced by the life context and situation in which we live. And finally, while we cannot ignore the Western theological heritage without very serious risk, at this stage in Christian history – when most Christians live outside of Europe – we must now put equal emphasis on theologies which have been created in Africa and Asia. To attempt to write such a Guide is something of a minefield, and I am sure that there will be many points at which readers are likely to disagree sharply with what has been written. However, this is all part of the risk of doing theology, and I hope that students may thereby be stimulated to try to answer some of the problems raised from their own context and experience.

Several colleagues from various parts of the world have kindly commented on the draft, and my thanks are especially due to Romy Tiongco and Professor Duncan Forrester, New College, Edinburgh; the Rev. Dr Otele Perelini, Malua Theological Seminary, Samoa and the Very Rev. Kirkley Sands, Dean of Templeton Seminary, Bahamas.

I am grateful to the editors of the ISG for undertaking a new imprint of this short Guide, which has given me the opportunity to add a brief discussion of postmodernism. While postmodernism is still mainly a European and American phenomenon, it has taken into its agenda a number of features which have been important in the development of theology in the wider world. The most notable of these are perhaps the open acknowledgement of the validity of a plurality of approaches to theology, and the need to challenge the claims to neutrality and objectivity of some theological traditions. A number of other corrections and alterations have been made to the text, mainly to bring it up to date.

JOHN PARRATT

Contents

Preface	vi
Using This Guide	xi
1. Getting Started	**1**
What is Theology?	1
Statements of Faith	3
Revelation	4
Reason	7
Who Does Theology?	8
Knowledge and Experience	9
Theology and the Church	10
Study Suggestions	11
2. The Language and Context of Theology	**13**
The Language of Theology	13
Metaphor, Symbol and Myth	14
The Changing Context of Theology	17
Putting the Gospel into New Contexts	19
Study Suggestions	21
3. The Bible	**23**
The Authority of the Bible	23
Principles for Understanding the Biblical Text	24
Ideological Readings of the Bible	26
The Literary Category	28
The Accuracy of the Biblical Text	31
Using the Bible in Doing Theology	32
Study Suggestions	33
4. The History of Theology	**35**
The Importance of the History of Christian Thought	35
Formation of the Canon	36
Liturgy and Creeds	37
Interpreting the Creeds	40
Relevance of Theological Movements	41

Later Statements of Faith	42
The Authority of the Church	42
The Impact of Western Philosophy and Science on Theology	43
The Importance of Third World Theology	44
Study Suggestions	45

5. Taking Account of Culture — 47

The Importance of Culture to Doing Theology	47
Culture: a Definition	48
Three Characteristics of Culture	49
Culture and Theology	51
An African Example of Cultural Theology	52
An Indian Example of Cultural Theology	53
Study Suggestions	54

6. Theologians in Society — 56

Social Groups	56
Social Control: Politics	57
Wealth and Production: Economics	57
Theologians as Members of Society	57
African and Indian Examples of Theology Addressing Racial Discrimination	59
An Example of Feminist Theology	61
African and Korean Examples of Theology Addressing Political Issues	62
A Latin American Example of Theology Addressing Economic Issues	64
Theology and World Economics	66
Study Suggestions	67

7. The Problem of History — 69

Linear and Cyclical Views of History	69
The Problem of the Accuracy of the Bible	70
Christian History	73
World History as Revelation	73
Interpreting History	75
Study Suggestions	76

8. Philosophies and Religions — 78

The Impact of Greek Thought on Early Christianity	78
Philosophy and Theology: Two Modern Examples	80

The Postmodern Condition	81
Philosophy and Theology: Indian and African Examples	84
Christian Theology and Non-Christian Religions	85
The Exclusivist Position	85
The Inclusivist Position	87
Mediating Positions	88
Study Suggestions	90
9. The Challenge of Doing Theology	**92**
Biblical Theology and Historical Theology	92
Systematic Theology	93
Creative Tension in Doing Theology	98
Study Suggestions	103
Further Reading	**104**
References	**107**
Glossary	**108**
Foreign Words and Phrases	117
Names	119
Key to Study Suggestions	**121**
Index	**124**

Using This Guide

The author in his Preface has indicated very clearly that the purpose of this Guide is not simply to provide factual information or ready-made infallible statements of faith or codes of practice. By offering pointers to some of the basic events, ideas and experiences which have informed and empowered the Churches and individual Christians over the centuries, he encourages readers to think out their own response to the call for theologically valid answers to the questions and issues encountered in their multifarious situations today.

STUDY SUGGESTIONS

Suggestions for further study appear at the end of each chapter. They are intended to help students understand more clearly what they have read, and to relate their studies to their own experiences of life and work in the world. They are grouped under three headings:
　1. *Words and Meanings*. These will help readers to check and deepen their understanding of any technical or other special terms used.
　2. *Review of Content*. These will help readers to review what they have read, and to ensure they have fully grasped and remembered the ideas discussed and information presented. Students may find it helpful to write down their answers and check them with the Key (p. 121).
　3. *Contextual Application and Discussion*. These not only indicate possible lines for further study, but will stimulate thoughtful readers to examine anew the basis of their own theological and religious assumptions, and the links between theology and action in their own and other Churches.

The *Key* will enable readers to check their own work on those questions which can be checked in this way. In most cases the Key does not supply the answer: it shows where an answer can be found.

Some tutors may wish to use these Study Suggestions selectively, or to substitute questions of their own. Some readers may not wish to follow them at all.

FURTHER READING

This section on p. 104 gives special recommendation of titles suggested for further reading, as a follow-up to each chapter.

REFERENCES

Details of books and articles quoted in each chapter are given on p. 107.

GLOSSARY

A Glossary giving outline definitions of technical and other specialist terms, which are asterisked at first appearance in the text, is provided on p. 108. Translations of foreign terms used are also given (p. 117), and brief background details of authors quoted and persons named (p. 119).

1
Getting Started

WHAT IS THEOLOGY?

For many people the very idea that we can talk about God is problematic. Many disciplines, especially the *natural sciences** – physics, chemistry and so on – take as their subject matter things which are concrete and observable. These subjects can be studied empirically*, that is, we can observe their raw materials with our physical senses. We may also, in certain cases, be able to put these materials under a microscope in a laboratory and carry out factual experiments which increase the observable data upon which we base our findings and conclusions. From these findings, which can be confirmed by anyone who will take the trouble to look, see and touch, we can construct our theories.

A similar method may be applied to some extent to the *human or social sciences*, those disciplines like sociology*, politics, economics and so on, which take human beings in society as their object and data. While human beings are far less predictable than the physical and chemical substances that provide the raw materials for the natural sciences, the observer of human nature or of people in societies can note behaviour patterns and reach findings that may reasonably be defended as correct. The *humanities* or arts disciplines – such as music, literature and painting – are rather less tangible. But while we may differ over what to make of a particular piece of music, poem or sculpture – our interpretation* or explanation of it – we cannot reasonably deny that it is *there*, that it exists. Events in history also, while we may not actually have witnessed them with our own eyes, can be verified to a greater or lesser extent by examining written documents or collecting oral sources.

In one sense theology stands apart from these disciplines by virtue of its subject matter, and is more akin to those speculative disciplines such as philosophy and (some would argue) mathematics. Not everyone believes there is a God, and therefore not everyone will be convinced that theologians are talking about something that is *real* in the sense that chemical substances, sculptures and people are real. Indeed someone has said that theology is the only discipline whose critics can deny that its subject matter really exists! The practice of theology, then, will be limited to those who believe in God in some way. It is, of course, possible for a non-believer to study what others have said about God;

but this is not doing theology but studying the history of religious thought – a valid discipline, but quite distinct from theology itself.

Theology, then, demands some kind of personal commitment, over and above the normal kind of commitment one would expect of any scholar in any discipline. It demands that we accept that the world of our senses is not the only reality there is, and that there is a supra-empirical* reality, a dimension of existence which goes beyond the physical world of the senses. There is certainly a difficulty here, and one which the theologian has to face squarely. For while we may firmly believe in what we have called supra-empirical reality we, like others before us, can only encounter it in this world.

To that extent (as we shall see) we cannot dismiss the empirical world as unimportant, unreal or anti-God. This was an error which some early Christian thinkers (the Christian Gnostics*) fell into: they believed that God, being absolutely pure, could have no contact whatsoever with a tainted evil world of matter. This is a position which Christian theology as a whole has firmly rejected. All our thinking about God has to take into account the assumption that the world is God's creation. Our theology will thus have to be large and comprehensive enough to embrace and relate to all aspects of the natural and human sciences – but at the same time without losing its particular convictions and insights.

Given, then, the assumption that *God is*, the next problem of theology is how He may be described. Theology is properly defined as *speaking about God*, from the two Greek words *theos** (God) and *logos** (word, or reasoned discourse). Of course, it is not only Christians who can practise theology. Hindus, Muslims, and indeed the adherents of any other faith which teaches there is a God, may also seek to express in logical terms what they believe, on the basis of their own tradition, scriptures and experiences. In this sense we can equally talk of Hindu theology or Muslim theology and so on. However, our aim in this book is to draw out guidelines for the specific task of Christian theology.

While we cannot avoid taking non-Christian religions into account in this task (see chapter 8) we shall be focusing only upon those factors which affect our doing theology as Christians. This necessarily involves taking up a particular position from the outset, that is, looking at God and the world from the standpoint of Christian commitment, as opposed to that of any other faith or philosophy.

Theology as 'speaking about God' can be understood in different ways. Some, more conservative* theologians have claimed that theology is a systematic description of God as He really is in His true nature. This is possible, so they would argue, because God has revealed Himself fully to human beings, especially in Scripture. Others would respond that this goes too far. While not minimizing the reality of revelation*, they would contend that the human mind can never fully grasp what God is really like. Theology, therefore, being a discipline done by human beings, cannot describe God as He is in His very essence, but only as we perceive Him to be. This is not to say that it is simply the opinions of human beings about God. On the contrary, so the argument goes, our perceptions about God depend upon His self-disclosure. But since the finite human mind is not capable of completely grasping the infinite God (as Augustine put it), and since God's revelation has to be expressed in human language, we can only speak in approximate terms of what God is like. Theology can therefore never be exact or infallible.

We shall in this Guide accept the second definition as the more reasonable, and *understand theology as our apprehension of God based on His self-revelation*. On the basis of this definition there will always be some room for disagreement between one theologian and another. There may, of course, be differences of opinion over what revelation itself consists of, and we shall return to this problem later. Almost certainly there will be differences over what this revelation means, what it seeks to tell us, and how it can be expressed in human language. That is, there will be conflicts over both the interpretation and the restatement of revelation.

STATEMENTS OF FAITH

During periods of controversy in the first five centuries, the Church drew up statements of faith which it (or at least sections of it) came to regard as definitive, that is, true and to be accepted by its adherents. The great ecumenical* creeds* (the Apostles' Creed, the Nicene and the Athanasian Creeds) are perhaps the best examples of this. It probably is important, from time to time, to try to define in formal statements what the essence of the Christian faith is, or rather is perceived to be. If this were not done, then there would presumably be no practical way of distinguishing what is Christian from what is not. But there are also serious problems involved in regarding such statements as tests of belief that are binding for all true Christians at all times and in all places.

For the modern Christian one problem is that such statements leave little space for creative thinking. If the Church (however we understand that term) defines for me what I as an individual Christian can and cannot believe, then I have little space for exploring my own experience of Christ within my own culture* and context*. I may indeed find that I cannot, in all conscience, accept, for example, parts of the creeds in their present form and terminology. Do I then cease to be Christian even though I have a real experience of Christ as Lord? For this reason many theologians have argued that the creeds should be understood as guidelines rather than as absolute definitions, and they give us only the broad parameters or boundaries of Christian belief.

Secondly, it can be pointed out that the Church as a whole has never been completely agreed as to a basic statement of the essence of the Christian faith – unless perhaps it was the very early and simple confession 'Jesus is Lord'. The Nicene Creed, for example, caused enormous controversy before it was agreed upon, and it was a controversy in which supporters of that Creed did not always behave better than their opponents! Furthermore, the three great divisions of Christendom – the Roman Catholic*, the Eastern Orthodox* and the Protestant – have deeply rooted differences which do not prevent them all being truly 'Christian'.

A more important fact, however, is that all such statements of faith are expressed in language and terminology which belong in time and are not eternal: they reflect a culture, language and outlook which are of their own time and cannot easily be transferred as they stand to other ages and cultures. They are, in other words, historically and culturally conditioned. The terms used in the Nicene Creed, for example, are drawn from a Greek philosophy which few but trained scholars can now understand. Therefore simply to repeat what that earlier generation said in the language and thought forms of its own time, and to expect that it will convey the same meaning to us today, is unrealistic. Our situation, context and mental outlook are all quite different.

What we are saying here is that no statement of faith is ever final and unchangeable; statements of faith have to be re-created, restated and reinterpreted in each different age and context if they are to be properly understood. This is surely what doing Christian theology is all about. It is, as Paul Tillich once said, the restatement of the meaning of the Christian faith for each and every age, and in terms which that age can readily understand.

REVELATION

We spoke above of the theologians working on the materials available to them and of God's 'self-disclosure'. Let us now try to examine these terms more closely. If the first basic assumption of Christian theologians is that *God is*, the second must be that *God discloses Himself to human beings*. That is, we accept not only the existence of God, but also His revelation of Himself to men and women. It is, of course, quite possible to believe that there is a God, and even that He created the universe, but to reject the idea that He is at all interested in human beings (this approach is often called deism*). The assumption of Christian theology, however, is that God by His very nature has a special relationship with human beings, and that revelation is part and parcel of that relationship.

But what do we mean by revelation? Most theologians would assume that there is an awareness of God which is open to everyone. This is often called 'general revelation', though some people are unhappy with this term and would not make a very sharp distinction between general revelation and what we shall call 'special revelation'. We shall return to this point in chapter 7.

There are several passages in the Bible which speak of God's revelation to all human beings in this general way. The Psalms, for example, speak of the glory of God which is traceable in creation (e.g. Ps. 8), and some of the prophets saw God's work in the history of non-Israelite peoples (e.g. Isa. 44.28—45.6; Amos 9.7). In the Gospels Jesus spoke of God's care for all (Matt. 5.45) and the writer of Acts represents Paul as arguing that there is a desire in all people to seek after God (Acts 17.21ff; compare Acts 14.15–17 and Rom. 1.18ff).

The term 'natural theology'* is often used to designate the knowledge of God as Creator, which is available to all human beings through the natural world. This knowledge, it is argued, is the starting-point from which we then go on to know God as Redeemer through the Gospel. Not all theologians have accepted this distinction, and Karl Barth in particular has opposed the very idea that natural theology is possible. He believed that revelation could only take place in Christ. However, general revelation does seem to be assumed in at least some passages of Scripture, and it seems to be reasonable to find a place for it in Christian belief.

More important for theology, however, is the idea that there is a particular revelation of God to a particular people at particular times and places (the term 'special revelation' is often used to describe this). God discloses Himself, it is argued, to and through His covenant people, in the history of Israel in the Old Testament period and in the Church in the New Testament. This biblical revelation is thus through specific 'elect' communities.

The idea of 'election'* may seem on the surface to be unfair and biased. However, this is not really the case if the biblical concept is properly understood. Biblical election is not so much election for privilege as for service, that is, so that through the elect people the revelation of God may be spread to all human beings. This idea is found in many places in the Old Testament, of which the Servant Song in Isaiah 42.1ff (originally referring to the nation of Israel) is but one example.

Since revelation of this kind is centred upon people it logically must take place through history. Concrete historical events, interpreted in Scripture by people of faith, are seen as occasions on which God shows Himself to human beings and through which He works out His saving purposes in the world. Not all events are regarded by biblical writers as equally important for revelation. In the Old Testament, revelation is grouped around a series of pivotal*, important happenings which are interpreted as having saving value. Such are the great ancient traditions of the Pentateuch* – the promise to the patriarchs, the Exodus, the wanderings in the wilderness, the giving of the Law, the occupation of Canaan – traditions which are interpreted and reinterpreted again and again by the Old Testament writers. The climactic* events of the kingdom of David and the fall of Jerusalem were added to this inventory of sacred history at a later date, and it is from these latter events that the messianic expectation developed. Similarly the Gospel is essentially rooted in the history of Jesus of Nazareth, His life and teaching, death and resurrection, which are reflected upon by the New Testament writers.

Whatever problems we may have with certain events in the biblical story (and theologians are not excused from struggling with the historical difficulties in the Bible), Christian theology is at root an attempt to give meaning to certain historical happenings. God's revelation is thus revelation through actual events, rather than a revelation of timeless philosophical ideas, and these events are understood as the acts of God in the liberation and redemption of His people and ultimately of all creation.

Theology, however, does not simply restate the events of the Bible. It has to attempt to find some sort of pattern and order in them, and to take from them principles or beliefs (dogmas*). So the Bible is a raw material of theology, but it does not present us with a systematic set of truths as it stands. It needs to be worked upon in order to draw out principles about the nature of God and His liberating activity, which are then to be formulated into a coherent pattern.

Most theologians would go on to argue that revelation did not cease when the canon of the New Testament (the collection of agreed sacred writings) was complete. They would also contend that the whole of the history of the Church, as the new people of God, also constitutes revelation. While there is truth in this claim, it raises a number of important questions to which we shall return in chapter 7. Perhaps the most pressing of these is how we can interpret and find meaning in the history of the Church. While the writers of the Scriptures are, to some extent, their own interpreters in that they reflect upon the meaning of the events they describe and draw their conclusions as to what God is saying through those events, we have no such guidelines in church history. Scripture is thus self-interpreting in a way in which the history of the Church can never be, and as individuals from different church traditions we shall probably often differ, perhaps quite radically, over what God is saying to us through the events of church history.

REASON

Theologians, then, are presented with the raw materials – general revelation, Scripture, church history – which they broadly accept as God's revelation to humanity. To make these raw materials coherent they then have to examine them, to sift and evaluate their relative importance, with all the critical resources at their disposal. These are activities of human reason.

Some great Christian thinkers have indeed tended to play down the importance of reason. Tertullian, writing in the third century, for example, once claimed 'I believe because it is impossible.' What he meant was that the Christian faith cannot be completely reduced to statements which are 'reasonable', for it is essentially something which comes from a God who is far beyond our fallible human minds. In other words, there are some things about faith which transcend reason, just as the 'supra-empirical reality' we experience and 'believe in' through faith transcends the empirical reality we 'know' through our physical senses.

There is indeed a valid point here. While it is true that reason is a major element in the human personality, it is not the only one, and there are some aspects of religion – love, for example, or mystical experience – which can neither be reduced to nor completely understood by reason. Thus, there will always be something transcendent* about the theological task.

Nevertheless, theology is a discipline which seeks to communicate itself and to be understood. Consequently it has to present a 'reasonable' account of Christian belief and convictions. We would also find it rather hard to believe in a God who asks us to accept things which are flatly contrary to the reason with which He has endowed us! If Christian theologians try to escape from reason they run the risk of making Christianity appear incredible and irrelevant. They have to work on the raw materials of revelation in such a way that their findings can be presented and set out in a manner which is not unreasonable. They will at the same time fully recognize that human reason cannot explain, or even grasp, everything about the nature of God. The claims of reason will involve us in an honest examination of the many difficulties we encounter in the sources of revelation, moral and historical difficulties in particular.

The claims of reason also mean that we have to try to relate revelation to the world in which we live, and to the possible objections to belief that come from the natural and human sciences. At the same time the theologians have to examine revelation, as each perceives it, from a particular context from which they cannot escape, that is, the context of their own life and experience and the life and experience of the

Church of which each is a part. Their task, then, is to relate what is 'given' in *revelation* to the 'given' of their own situation in a concrete and particular historical, social and cultural *context*. These are the two *foci* of any theology that hopes to speak to its own time. We shall examine these in more detail in the following chapters.

WHO DOES THEOLOGY?

Let us now move from the discipline of theology to the doer: who does, or can do, Christian theology? In one sense, of course, all Christian believers 'do' theology in one way or another. All our worship, prayer, reflection on the Scriptures, even our informal conversation about the Christian faith with each other, is doing theology. More important, the daily living of Christians, especially in their involvement individually or collectively in striving for justice and the welfare of their fellow human beings, is theological action – 'praxis'*, to use the term made familiar to us by Latin American liberation theology*.

It is indeed becoming increasingly recognized, particularly in those countries where there are varying degrees of literacy, that such non-written or 'oral theology'* is an important ground-work from which a more structured and sophisticated theology emerges. But we must at the same time be careful not to exaggerate the role of oral theology as a creative force. Whatever emerges from the Christian community will usually do so because of gifted individuals within that community (whether literate or illiterate) and will then need to be reflected upon, refined and written down before it can become generally accessible to the Church as a whole.

Usually theology is understood as systematic reflection upon the meaning of Christian faith, rather than the spontaneous expression of that faith (as is oral theology). This is certainly the impression one gets when reading the New Testament Epistles, which seek to explain the meaning of belief and its practical consequences in a well-argued way.

Doing theology in a creative way thus assumes a fair degree of knowledge and understanding, both of the sources of revelation and of the context in which theologians operate. A defective understanding of the former will lead to a theology which is detached from its fundamental historic roots; too little attention to the latter may lead to a kind of orthodoxy* which is irrelevant to the world in which we live. Some African Independent Churches have been accused of the first fault; some fundamentalist* movements believing in the literal truth of the Bible, of the second.

KNOWLEDGE AND EXPERIENCE

Basically, then, theologians – like the practitioners of any other discipline – must possess sufficient knowledge of their subject matter if they are to be able to say anything worthwhile. But knowledge by itself is not enough.

The New Testament writers, when they speak about the knowledge of the Christian, often use the Greek word *epignosis** in preference to the normal one *gnosis**. *Epignosis* has been paraphrased as 'knowledge by experience': it is not simply intellectual head knowledge, but rather knowledge as apprehended by the whole person, the heart and will as well as the mind. Theologians speak as much from within their own experience of God as they do from their knowledge of Scripture and tradition. This is because our knowledge of God does not exist as an abstraction. It cannot be separated from the perceivers; that is, it can only be understood as part of our own human response to God. While it is true that God speaks to us in revelation, that revelation must itself be apprehended and received by the person to whom it is addressed. Our religious experience, then, is the medium through which the primal sources of revelation speak to each of us, as the word of God becomes actual and alive to me as an individual person.

The German theologian Schleiermacher has often been criticized for speaking of religion as a 'feeling of absolute dependence'. But what he meant was far from simply emotion. It was rather a sense of wonder and immediate awareness of the transcendent God, a response of the whole person, mind and will as well as heart. In Christian theology this is our response to a revelation which as it were, finds us or meets us, and answers our deepest concerns. It is this kind of religious experience which is the basis for doing Christian theology.

Put another way, theology demands a personal commitment, for theologians carry on their work on the basis of a conviction of the essential truth of the Christian message. Paul Tillich described this as 'working from within the theological circle'. Theologians are trying to make explicit their own convictions about the Christian faith; it is (in Anselm's words) 'faith seeking understanding'. For this reason it is not possible for, say, a Muslim or an atheist to 'do' Christian theology. While they may study it and arrive at an informed opinion about it, they cannot create it. This can be done only from within, from a standpoint of commitment to the truth and validity of the Christian faith.

Does this mean that Christian theology is for the internal consumption of Christian believers only, and that it has nothing to say to the non-Christians? Some have indeed taken this position, that Christian theology is essentially Christians talking to Christians about Christ. It is certainly true that theology is only fully meaningful to those who are, with the theologians, within the theological circle, that is, within the Church in its broadest sense (even though they may not share all the details of Christian belief in the same way).

There is, however, an approach to theology which seeks to address the interested outsider, and tries to justify the reasonableness of the Christian message to the unbelievers. This is often called apologetics*. It was the kind of thing Tillich was trying to do when he argued that all people have an 'ultimate concern' which is basically religious, and that therefore all of us, believers and non-believers alike, have a common religious dimension to our existence which finds its fulfilment in God. Apologetic theology looks for common ground between the Christian faith and non-Christian ideologies* and experiences. On the whole, however, theology is usually understood in its more restricted sense of a reasonable statement of the Christian faith by believers for believers.

THEOLOGY AND THE CHURCH

If this last statement is accepted, it logically follows that theology is done within the Christian community, the Church. Though theologians do, and indeed must, speak as individuals (and for that reason they are seldom in complete agreement with each other), they also speak as members of a community. In so doing they draw upon a common deposit of tradition – they speak out of the Church and (primarily at any rate) they speak to the Church.

As we have seen, the creative theologians will almost certainly go beyond the mere repetition of the Church's traditions and statements of faith. They will probably defend to some degree the tradition out of which they work, but they will also, if they are to make any useful contribution to our contemporary understanding of the Christian faith, challenge the Church continually to rethink its position. At times they may well, therefore, be unpopular and may even be regarded as troublesome freethinkers. But it is a fact of Christian history that what has been regarded as outrageous heresy by one generation has often been commonly accepted by the next as part of the Church's tradition.

Creative theologians will always, as it were, be a step ahead of their time. Of course, not all their ideas will be accepted, or even be worth accepting, and much theology which creates a stir when it first appears sooner or later falls into a well-deserved oblivion. The common wisdom of the Church, as the body of Christ which possesses the Spirit of truth, will test, approve, or reject. The important thing is that doing theology ought to present a continual challenge to Christians to understand and express their faith in new ways which are in tune with their age and context.

STUDY SUGGESTIONS

WORDS AND MEANINGS

1. (a) Give examples of disciplines or subjects of study under each of the following headings:
     (i) natural sciences;
     (ii) human sciences;
     (iii) arts subjects.
   (b) In what chief way do all these disciplines differ from theology as a subject of study?
2. Explain what is meant by:
   (a) 'supra-empirical reality';
   (b) 'human beings are less predictable than physical or chemical substances';
   (c) 'culturally and historically conditioned';
   (d) 'the theological circle'.
3. Give a brief description of each of the following:
   (a) sense data;
   (b) deism;
   (c) oral theology;
   (d) apologetics.
4. How would you answer someone who asked you to define theology?

REVIEW OF CONTENT

5. What are some of the main differences in method between studying the sciences and doing theology? What, if any, are the similarities?
6. Why is it that theology can only provide approximate descriptions of what God is like?
7. What, according to the writer of this book, are the two *foci* or 'givens' which have to be related in doing theology?
8. What are the differences between general revelation and special revelation?
9. What two different sorts of knowledge are required in doing theology?

CONTEXTUAL APPLICATION AND DISCUSSION

10. Do you agree with the statement that 'no theology is ever final'? If not, why not?
11. In what way are events in history important for theology?
12. What part does human reason play in doing theology?
13. 'Knowledge of God [. . .] can only be understood as part of our own human response to God' (p. 9). What is your opinion?

14 How would you answer someone who claimed that because we cannot experience God with our physical senses, therefore He cannot exist?

2
The Language and Context of Theology

THE LANGUAGE OF THEOLOGY

We said above that theology is reasonable communication about God to others. Theologians are therefore obliged to communicate through human speech and language, inadequate though this often may be. How can we communicate when talking about God? What kind of language can we use?

Most disciplines have their specialist vocabularies, which may not immediately be understood by outsiders untrained in those disciplines. Physicists talk about 'neutrons' (and even 'gluons'), anthropologists about 'matrilineal' and 'virilocal' societies, musicians about 'modes' and 'keys', and so on. There is an element of technical language in any discipline. This is not intended to mystify non-experts, but rather to allow practitioners to communicate their ideas in a compact and systematic way. Theology is no exception, and theologians will therefore need to familiarize themselves with terminology which is a kind of shorthand, and which enables them to say in a precise and brief way what otherwise might involve lengthy and cumbersome explanation. Two mistakes need to be avoided: first, technical expressions should be defined carefully. We should understand clearly what we mean when we use terms like 'eschatology'*, 'soteriology'*, 'existential'*, and so on – the use of such technical language should not be a cover for imprecise and woolly thinking! And second, theologians should resist the temptation to lapse into a kind of esoteric* language which can be understood only by experts. The Christian Gospel is, after all, first and foremost a 'proclamation' of good news, and it should never become so esoteric and specialized that it excludes intelligent and sympathetic outsiders.

Theology faces from the outset a language problem that it shares with few other disciplines. Theological language cannot, because of the nature of its subject matter, be 'scientific'. Though it may draw some of its data from what may be seen and heard with the physical senses, it is fundamentally concerned with what we called earlier the 'supra-empirical'. Theology therefore cannot use language simply in its normal or literal sense. In order to express what is ultimately inexpressible in human speech, theology has to use figures of speech, metaphor*, symbol* and poetry.

There is one view which regards all statements which cannot be proved by the senses as meaningless, literally 'non-sense'. This is the assumption of the crude popular materialism*, which claims that the only things which really exist are those which we can see, touch and hear – the philosophy that 'seeing is believing'. It is also the assumption of a sophisticated system of philosophy which came to be known as linguistic philosophy* or *logical positivism**. There are many serious problems with this point of view. Quite apart from the fact that we cannot always trust our physical senses (a colour-blind man, for example, does not see 'true' colours), this view makes the very big assumption that everything that is real can be examined and verified by the human physical senses.

This is obviously a most inadequate position for anyone who believes that there is a God. The view that language is meaningful only if it refers to things that can be proved by the senses, then, will not do for theology. It is also clear that perception and understanding can take place on a number of different levels. The words on this page can (rightly) be understood as paper and ink. This is true as far as it goes, but it clearly does not go far enough. The ultimate meaning of the words is to be understood on quite a different plane, on the level of the ideas that a particular set of paper and ink symbols (words) is meant to convey.

METAPHOR, SYMBOL AND MYTH

What then is the peculiar nature of theological or religious language? Every reader of the Bible is aware that its writers often use non-literal language. John, for example, tries to convey the significance of Jesus by statements such as 'I am the bread of life' or 'I am the light of the world'. No one would dream of taking these statements literally. We accept that in these metaphorical statements John is using powerful symbols which convey in a short and effective way what would otherwise take whole paragraphs. These statements are the more striking simply because they use symbols, for symbols force us to sit up and take notice (in a way that 'ordinary' speech often does not) and think about the inner significance of the statement in question. John's symbols are drawn from a particular context, that of the Jewish and Greek thought of the first century, and we shall appreciate their full import better, the more knowledge we have of this particular context – though perhaps the most striking thing about these particular symbols, light and bread, is that they have a near universal significance and are therefore able to speak with similar power to us in our own, quite different, context.

Paul also uses metaphors or figures of speech which are drawn from the life and world of his time. This is evident, for example, when he seeks to explain the meaning of Christian salvation. When he writes of the Christian being 'redeemed' he is borrowing language from the ancient slave market, which described the 'redemption' or 'buying back' of the slave into liberty. Similarly, 'justification'* is a metaphor taken from the law courts and meant literally the setting free of the accused. 'Reconciliation' again is probably a metaphor taken from warfare, when former enemies agree upon a peace settlement. Like John, Paul is not using this language in its literal sense. He is rather arguing that there are certain aspects of Christian salvation which may be illustrated by what happens when slaves are released, the accused are set free, a peace is agreed between enemies, and so on. He is describing the spiritual experience of the Christians in their relationship to God in language and metaphors which his first-century readers could readily understand.

Today, of course, we seldom speak in such terms because we do not share the same social and political world as Paul. Consequently, the full import of his metaphors does not hit us with the same impact until we try to put ourselves into the situation of Paul's first readers and try to imagine what the metaphor meant to them in their own age and context.

Thus Christian theologians always have to seek for symbols and metaphors which are readily understandable within their own cultural and social context. Such symbols will probably be different from those used by the New Testament writers and from those commonly used in Christian tradition. The most effective religious symbols are those which communicate themselves immediately to our experience, some of which – like light, bread, water – are, as we have seen, equally valid in many different ages and contexts. These symbols are not just arbitrary signs, like for example red as a colour signifying 'stop' or 'danger', when some other bright colour might do just as well. Symbols like those mentioned above actually convey an immediate meaning; they (as Tillich once put it) share in the reality they seek to communicate. As such they speak not only to the intellect but also, perhaps primarily, to the heart and the experience of every person.

Some symbols derive their force from their association with historical events. The cross, as a symbol of salvation, is immediately associated in the mind of Christians with an event in the past. But as a symbol the cross means more than just an event. It also conveys the significance and meaning of that event, namely the crucifixion of Jesus as the source of forgiveness and the symbol of new life. The empty tomb would also be an equally valid symbol for the latter.

We have so far used the terms 'metaphor' and 'symbol' almost interchangeably, and it is indeed not very easy to make a sharp distinction between them in theological language. It will be helpful at this point to look also at another term which has been widely used in theological discourse, namely 'myth'*. The German theologian Bultmann, in an essay published in 1941, caused a great stir in the theological world by using this term in the context of the New Testament. For him the language of the New Testament was 'mythological', that is, couched in picture language which reflected the world-view of the first century, a world-view which we cannot today share. He pointed to the idea of the three-storeyed universe (heaven, earth, the underworld), of the world of spirits which superimpose themselves on humans, to the concept of the redeemer-figure who descends from heaven, and so on. For Bultmann this mythological world-view was not an essential part of the New Testament message, but only a 'shell' which had to be stripped away (he coined the term 'demythologized'*, de-mythed) in order to reveal the essence of the New Testament Gospel, the *kerygma** or preached message.

Many people felt that Bultmann had gone too far in attributing pictorial language to the New Testament and that he was in danger of demythologizing the message along with the language. A few (like Bonhoeffer) thought he had not gone far enough and asked why he did not demythologize the concept of God as well! We shall not attempt to enter into these arguments here (readers who are interested in this debate can study Bultmann and his critics and make up their own minds). Here I want only to make two points about the use of theological language which Bultmann's work highlighted.

The first is that we cannot deny that a very great deal of biblical and theological language is metaphorical, symbolical (Tillich's word) or mythical (Bultmann's). To take all biblical and theological language as literal is quite simply to misunderstand what the authors were trying to say, and seriously to compromise ourselves as theologians.

Secondly, however, we do need to 'draw the line' between symbolical and literal language somewhere. Some biblical statements are obviously meant to be taken in their literal sense, for Christianity is usually (and rightly) understood as a faith which is based on certain facts. Theologians will differ among themselves as to where to draw the line between symbolical and literal statements, and such disagreements are inevitable and probably necessary for creative theology.

What we have to accept if theological dialogue is to be fruitful is that the most radical 'demythologizers', quite as much as the most rigid 'literalists'*, are genuinely seeking to grapple with the question of what the essence of the Christian faith is for us today, and to express that faith in terms which they see as the most meaningful to us. It may well be that some of the supposed sharp differences between theologians of various traditions is less a matter of the substance of the faith than of the form or language in which it is expressed.

All theologians have to work within their own language and social context* when they try to express their understanding of the Christian faith. Theology is essentially struggling to express in a contemporary and contextual way what we believe and experience about God. It will not be enough simply to repeat biblical or traditional Christian statements and expect them to be meaningful to Christians in our world today. On the contrary, symbols, language and thought-forms from the Church's own present-day context will have to be used if the Christian message is to be clearly presented and understood. Theologians in many parts of the non-Western world are now addressing this task, and we shall refer to some of them in subsequent chapters.

THE CHANGING CONTEXT OF THEOLOGY

We have already referred to the 'context' of theology. Each one of us lives within a specific historical, social, political and cultural context. This forms a 'given' within which we must live our lives and, however much we would wish to, we cannot (unless we completely abandon our family, home and country) escape from this history and environment. Theology, like any other human discipline, is therefore always carried out within a particular and specific context. It is not something which exists eternally in the heavens and descends to earth untouched and unmarked by the human condition. On the contrary, it is something which emerges from that condition and it cannot avoid reflecting the historical and cultural context in which it is done. To say this is to say that there is no such thing as a 'final' theology: theology is always 'in the making'. It is never static, it is always adapting itself and being adapted to new and ever-changing historical contexts.

A glance at the origins of Christianity will illustrate this. The Christian faith arose within a particular historical context, that of the Palestinian world of the Roman Empire. Its founder, Jesus, belonged to that world and expressed Himself through the thought-forms of that world. There was no other way, humanly speaking, that He could communicate and be understood by His followers. The terms and ideas that Jesus used in His teaching – terms like Messiah, Son of Man, Kingdom of God, ideas such as covenant, law and eschatology – were to a large extent determined by the religious and cultural experience and background of Jesus Himself and His hearers. This fact is one reason why the synoptic Gospels are at times so difficult for us to understand, for they come to us today wrapped up, as it were, in the garments of first-century Palestinian Judaism. To that extent Jesus also (as one famous theologian put it) 'appears to us as a stranger and an enigma to our time'.

What happened when the Gospel broke through the boundaries of Palestine? Could the same language and thought-forms be used? Clearly not. For one thing the preaching of Jesus was in Aramaic, while most of the early preachers of Christianity used Greek, the common language of the eastern part of the Roman empire. Now all translation involves some loss and some modification of meaning. There are very few words which have an exact equivalent in another language (especially when those languages, like Aramaic and Greek, have such different structures). So what became most important was not so much the individual words as the meaning behind those words. A simple 'word for word' translation would not do justice to the true meaning.

The only title Jesus is described in the Gospels as using to refer to himself is 'Son of Man'. In Aramaic this apparently had a fairly well-defined meaning: rendered into Greek (as indeed into English) the phrase is a meaningless tautology – it seems to say the same thing twice over. Consequently, as far as we can tell, Paul never used this term when writing to the Greek-speaking Gentile Christians. He had to find other titles – symbols in the sense we discussed in the last section – which were familiar to the experience of his readers, but which would convey the same idea as 'Son of Man'. The term he most often used is *kurios**: Lord. So appropriate was this term that it passed into the liturgy and confessions of the early Church.

Again, when Paul speaks of the death of Jesus or of baptism, he does not often do so in the language and symbols of Palestinian Judaism, though he himself understood these perfectly well. More often he turned to the language of the social customs, Greek philosophy and mystery* cults which were part of the world and experience of his converts. Meaning had to be clothed in the terminology of the culture and background of the hearers. The words and deeds of Jesus were thus 'translated' or reinterpreted so that the unfamiliar language and symbols of their original setting were replaced by those which suited the situation of the receivers. The old language was re-created and re-thought to suit new contexts.

Theology has always and everywhere to follow this principle. It is an ongoing task as theologians continually rethink and re-experience their faith in terms of their own age and context. It is therefore a never-ending task; as the context continually changes, so the language and expression of theology must change.

NEW CONTEXTS
PUTTING THE GOSPEL INTO NEW CONTEXTS

The implication of this for non-Western cultures is clear. The Western world has experienced Christianity for such a long period that the language and symbols of the Bible and Christian tradition have become part and parcel of Western culture. This is not the case with Asia, Africa or the Pacific. Consequently believers in the newer Churches have to explore and experiment in expressing the truths of the Gospel in the language and symbols of their own culture.

Does this mean that we are trying to express an unchangeable and eternal truth in constantly changing and temporal language? Some theologians have indeed argued along these lines, that the essence of Christian theology is unchangeable and that only the form in which it is expressed changes. On this view theology is a timeless truth, an unchanging 'body' which needs simply to be 're-clothed' in modern dress whether European, Asian, African or whatever. This view looks convincing enough, and probably there would be few who would deny that there is a core to the Christian message which is valid for all peoples in all ages and cultures. But the issue is rather more subtle than this.

The problem is that the 'core' or 'kernel' of the Gospel has never existed, and can never exist, in abstraction outside a particular and specific context. To pursue our metaphor, there is never a 'naked body' of the Gospel which does not wear the clothes of one or other culture. As we have seen above, even the message of Jesus or of Paul was expressed not in timeless terms but in terms of the religious cultures and situations of their own time and place. Thus every time we try to define the 'essence of the Gospel' we cannot avoid doing so in terms of our own quite specific context.

This, as we have said, is not to deny that there is an eternally valid body of truth in Christianity. It is rather to say that we can only perceive and describe this truth as clothed in our own historically conditioned language and culture. Every expression of the Gospel into another context thus involves the use of the tongues and dialects of that context. Words in vernacular languages for concepts like God, sin, salvation and so on, have to be used.

It is well known that many of the Western missionaries used the traditional names for the Supreme Being when they came to translate 'God' in the Bible and in their preaching. While there was little alternative for terms like, for example, *Mlungu** or *Modimo**, these terms did not, and could not, correspond exactly to what the Bible means by *JHWH** or *theos** (itself a word borrowed from Greek religion). All these terms are to a greater or lesser extent culturally conditioned. While it is true that a Christian content may in time have been given to traditional names for God, there inevitably remains also a certain traditional content, the more so since, in many parts of Asia, Africa and the Pacific, these same terms have continued to be used for the traditional deity.

What we are saying here is that translation from one language to another always involves some change in meaning. Even though a good translation deepens meaning for the recipient, it is also often true that pre-Christian overtones of meaning may at the same time remain. The problem becomes particularly acute when it comes to translating the term 'Holy Spirit'. In China Catholics and Protestants use different Chinese characters for the same concepts and the Chinese have come to regard the two differing Christian traditions as separate religions.

Doing theology, then, involves a sense of discovery. Starting from the original sources of tradition, theology is discovering for ourselves what Christ means to us, and expressing that meaning in terms of our own language, culture and context. It is expressing creatively the significance of the Christian tradition at the point of our own experience.

Here, then, are the two poles of Christian theology. On the one hand there is Christian tradition, found primarily in the Scriptures and the history of the Church's doing theology for the past two thousand years. On the other hand there is our experience here and now in our particular concrete historical context. Theologians (or schools of theology) are not agreed as to how much weight should be placed on each, not even at which pole we should begin. But all are agreed that both are of vital importance. If we concentrate exclusively on the first pole, we shall run the risk of producing an academic theology which is cut off from the real world in which we live; if we concentrate only on the second, we run the equally dangerous risk of cutting ourselves off from our Christian roots and perhaps of distorting the Christian message.

Doing theology, therefore, is something of a delicate balancing act. So it is not to be expected, nor even to be desired, that we should have one theology which can be agreed by all Christians at all times and in all places. On the contrary, a valid expression of the Christian faith for our world demands that there should be a multiplicity of theologies. This is not a drawback. Rather it is a demonstration that *the Gospel of Jesus Christ is the word of God for salvation to all human beings in all times and contexts*. Genuine Christian theology is always situational and contextual, it meets us in our own particular situation and it springs from the context in which we find ourselves.

In the following chapters we shall firstly examine the sources of Christian theology, the Bible and the history of the Church's doing theology. Then in the remaining chapters we shall devote our attention to those main factors which go to make up the context in which the theologians do their work.

STUDY SUGGESTIONS

WORDS AND MEANINGS
1. (a) What is the difference between a 'metaphor' and a 'symbol'? Give an example of each.
   (b) What is meant by the word 'myth'?
2. Explain what is meant by:
   (a) esoteric;
   (b) situational and contextual;
   (c) a meaningless tautology.

REVIEW OF CONTENT
3. What is the particular 'language problem' which theologians have to face?
4. Why do we need to use 'figures of speech' in doing theology?
5. What is meant by 'demythologizing', and why do some theologians say it is necessary?
6. Explain what is meant by each of the following statements:
   (a) 'All translation involves some change in meaning';
   (b) 'Our world demands that there should be a multiplicity of theologies'.

CONTEXTUAL APPLICATION AND DISCUSSION
7. By what criteria or standards can we judge which terms or statements in the Bible are literal and which are figurative?
8. What names or titles for Creator God or Supreme Being were used among your people before the coming of Christianity? Were they adopted by Christian missionaries, and if so how far, if at all, has their meaning been changed as a result?
9. What symbols or metaphors from the language or culture of your country could be used to describe:
   (a) God;
   (b) Christ;
   (c) Christian salvation?
10. Some theologians argue that 'the essence of Christian theology is a timeless truth, independent of the language or culture in which it is presented'. If so, how do you think it could be identified?
11. Do you agree that there should be a multiplicity of theologies? If so, what should they have in common?
12. In what ways have the nationality and language of the first Christian

missionaries to your country influenced the development of the Church(es) there?
13 What are some of the problems of doing theology in the languages of areas where there is no existing Christian tradition?

3
The Bible

THE AUTHORITY OF THE BIBLE

All Christian Churches accept that the Bible is authoritative, that is, that it is the foundation document of the Christian faith. We show this allegiance to the Bible, for example, in our worship, by the public reading of Scripture, and (usually) by a sermon which is based (however remotely) on a biblical text. But what do we mean when we speak of the Bible as 'authoritative', or as the 'Word of God', or as 'inspired'?

Fundamentalist Christians would argue that to say that the Bible is inspired means that the very words were, as it were, spoken by God and that the Bible is therefore absolutely without errors. Logically this would have to mean the Bible in the original Hebrew and Greek text. But this position immediately raises a problem, for in many parts of the Bible (especially the Old Testament) this 'original' text is no longer fully recoverable with absolute certainty, and the textual critics (see below) have a hard task deciding, on the basis of the evidence available, just what the most likely original text really was. (Nonetheless, the evidence we have for the original biblical texts compares very favourably with that for other texts from the ancient world.) While most of the problematic texts in the Bible are not crucial for matters of belief, there is nevertheless something very unsatisfactory about the idea of a verbally inspired text of which we cannot now be completely certain.

Then there are the many historical difficulties in the Bible, those passages where the text does not match up to what is otherwise known from extra-biblical ancient writings, or from the findings of archaeology. Again, the Bible raises moral issues which would seem to militate against its being the exact words of God – problems like how a loving God could demand the extermination of the Canaanites or the execution of a whole family for the sin of one member. Perhaps most problematic of all for the idea of a verbally inspired Bible are the internal discrepancies within the Bible itself – either between different books which give varying accounts of the same event (conflicts between the historical books of the Old Testament, for example, or different Gospels in the New), or within individual books themselves (so-called 'doublets': that is, different accounts of the same event within the same biblical book).

We shall not here enter into these problems in detail – they are properly the task of biblical 'Introductions', and readers may refer to these if they wish to pursue this issue. Our present point is simply that the kind of fundamentalist approach to Scripture which regards it as the inerrant words spoken by God Himself is not very convincing and intellectually not very honest. And indeed there is no reason why it should be.

While the literalist position certainly has played a role in Christian history, it was never the only view of Scripture. Several of the church Fathers (and, for the Old Testament, early Jewish commentators) used the text of the Bible with a great deal more freedom, and some of the literary problems raised by the text of the Bible were pointed out very early on in the Christian era. The fundamentalist approach, as we know it, is in fact a fairly recent Western one, which was transplanted to the non-Western world during the heyday of the missionary expansion. Unfortunately it has persisted and has tended to hinder, rather than help, the development of indigenous theologies. A misunderstanding as to the nature of the biblical text tends to lead to misunderstandings as to its meaning.

Another, related, approach to the Bible is to regard it as the Word of God which speaks to us directly as we read and meditate upon it. One might call this a 'pietist' approach to Scripture. Now there is clearly an important truth in this position, and it should not be underestimated. Probably most Christians have experienced comfort or challenge from Scripture in this way. But aside from the fact that such experiences are usually intensely personal – and may be few and far between – they do not uncover the meaning of the Scripture as a whole, nor even, to the fullest extent, the meaning of individual texts. And indeed it is quite possible that our personal experience of a text will completely misunderstand its real import. As one scholar has put it, the Bible does not speak to our present situation as though the two thousand or more years intervening did not exist; it speaks directly only to the men and women of its own time. Before it can speak to us with the same clarity and in the same way, its meaning for the people of its own time needs to be carefully examined.

PRINCIPLES FOR UNDERSTANDING THE BIBLICAL TEXT

There are two basic principles which are essential for an understanding of the biblical text. The first is to recognize the literary form or category* of writing which is employed. When we are reading a novel, say, or a play, we do not approach it in the same way as we would a serious historical study. We recognize that the novelists or playwrights, though they may use a 'historical' background and even 'real' people, have a certain amount of freedom as to how they use their materials. The fact that Shakespeare's *Richard II* or *Macbeth* do not keep very closely to the historical facts does not bother us: the meaning of these works does not depend on a rigid adherence to the facts of history. 'Meaning' in these plays lies in the author's poetic and psychological exploration of the motives, feelings, thoughts and actions of the characters depicted.

Again, if we are reading a poem, we do not expect the literal meaning of the words used to be uppermost. The poet will use symbols, metaphors, word-pictures and so on, and indeed will often use language in quite new and striking ways. Tagore's *Gitanjali* or Oket p'Bitek's *The Song of Lawino* cannot be read in the same way as a textbook of biology! In practice, we usually come to different sorts of literature mentally prepared to understand them for what they are. The 'literary category', then, is all important for our understanding of the meaning of a piece of writing.

A second principle is to recognize the cultural and historical background of the work. To understand fully a novel like, say, *War and Peace*, we should ideally need to know something about social and political conditions in Russia during the nineteenth century, and especially about the conditions of the peasants and the life of the nobility. It would also help us to appreciate the book better if we knew something about Tolstoi and his own attitude to these issues. Similarly, if we are reading Ngugi's *The River Between* or Chinua Achebe's *Things Fall Apart*, we are unlikely to gain more than superficial benefit from them unless we know something about the cultural and religious customs of Kenya or Nigeria and a little about the problems of adjustment in Africa to the impact of colonialism and Christianity. In saying this, we can still recognize that readers can get a lot out of such books, and of the Bible likewise, even without a great deal of background knowledge. All the same, the full meaning of a piece of literature only begins to become clear when we take into account its cultural and historical background and the aims of the author.

The same principles apply to our understanding of the Bible. The questions we have alluded to above – the category of literature to which the writing belongs, the time of writing, the social, cultural and historical background, the aims of the author – are all part of what is termed 'biblical criticism'* or 'higher criticism' (in distinction from 'textual criticism'*, which we will look at below). The word 'criticism' is used here not, of course, in its popular sense of 'finding fault with', but in its primary meaning of 'careful examination and judgement'. What the higher critics try to do is to understand the Bible against its original time of writing and to try to discover what a text meant to the men and women of its own time.

This is a first essential step to the use of the Bible in doing theology. Failure to do this can lead to distorting results, and to using (and often to misusing) a text simply because it suits our own ideas. A sacramentalist*, for example, might interpret 1 John 2.20 in terms of literal anointing with oil after baptism, where a Pentecostal might see in it support for a charismatic experience; Episcopalians and Presbyterians might appeal to the same texts in support of their different types of church government; liberation theology appeals to the Exodus narrative, which an earlier generation of Afrikaners used to justify their occupation of the Transvaal. Obviously, if we so wish, we can use the Bible to support almost any position. This is a great danger in doing theology.

If they are to avoid misusing Scripture it is essential for theologians, as far as they possibly can, to determine the original meaning of a biblical passage, what it meant in the first place to the original speakers and hearers. This is often a very difficult task, but it is one that must not be shirked. As Calvin once put it: 'It is the first business of the interpreter to let the author say what he does say, instead of attributing to him what we think he ought to say.' He goes on: 'It is an audacity akin to sacrilege to use the Scriptures at our pleasure and to play with them as with a tennis ball.'

Before we can use Scripture for theological or dogmatic purposes, therefore, we are duty bound to find out as far as possible what it meant to the speaker or writer of a text and to the people who first heard or read it. Only when we have discovered that can we go on to ask what, if anything, the text can mean for ourselves and for the Church of our time. There is thus a twofold process in the use of the Bible in theology. The first is exegesis*, determining the meaning of the text in its original context; the second may be called hermeneutics*, the interpretation of that text for our own time and situation.

IDEOLOGICAL READINGS OF THE BIBLE

Some theologians have argued that the first task is not really possible because we cannot put ourselves back into the situation of the original hearers, and in any case none of us can be fully objective, that is, free of our prejudices and presuppositions. Consequently they argue that the interpretation of a biblical text can only be done from a particular ideological framework. This means that each interpreter has to see the text through the lenses of a particular theory which he or she accepts as true.

It must be recognized that ideological readings of the Bible have an important role to play in exposing the shortcomings of commonly accepted understandings of Scripture which are, erroneously, believed to be neutral and objective. Perhaps the most striking example of this in our own time has been that of Latin American theology of liberation. The hermeneutic of liberation theology has focused attention in a forceful way on the role of poor and oppressed people in the Bible, and has well demonstrated that the 'option for the poor' is an integral part of the biblical approach to salvation history (for example Isaiah 61.1, Luke 4.18).

A rather different kind of 'liberation theology' has been developed by feminist theologians. They argue, rightly, that Christian thought has, by and large, ignored the place of women in society, and that sometimes the biblical texts themselves can be described as patriarchal* and androcentric, that is, written for males and from a male perspective. Feminist approaches to the Bible seek to restore women into Christian history and theology, to read behind the text, as it were, and to show how women's concerns and women themselves can be given their rightful place in Christian thinking. Elisabeth Schüssler Fiorenza's rereading of St John's Gospel is a convincing example of this kind of hermeneutic.

Other feminist theologians would go further, and would argue that the language of Christian theology is itself tainted by male sexual bias, and that therefore the whole discourse of theology should be radically rethought, and that the 'femininity of God' should become a central concern. The linguistic issue of whether we should speak of God as 'He' may indeed be less relevant to some African and Asian cultures. These may give a much wider and richer attribution of feminine characteristics to God than is usually the case in the West, and do not necessarily use an explicitly masculine pronoun when speaking of God.

Such readings of Scripture remind us of two very important issues. The first is how far the New Testament writers did, consciously or unconsciously, accept the common attitudes of their time with regard to the position of the poor, of women, of slaves and so on. We need to take account of this when interpreting their writings. In other words, we shall have to try to distinguish between what in the New Testament is really normative for us today and what, on the other hand, is part of the cultural bias of a past age.

But secondly, we shall also have to be open to the possibility that early Christianity really was revolutionary with regard to certain aspects of society. No reputable commentator today would fail to emphasize the importance of the poor in the New Testament, and it is becoming increasingly clear that at least some of the New Testament traditions can be interpreted as showing that women played a far greater role in early Christianity than has commonly been acknowledged.

So there is certainly an element of truth in ideological approaches to Scripture. No one of us can be completely objective. We all see reality (including the reality of the Bible) through our own eyes, and we cannot pluck out our eyes in order to see straight! Thus ideological readings of the Bible can be a valuable corrective in exposing the shortcomings of commonly accepted understandings of the Scriptures.

Nevertheless, there are some serious problems in arguing that hermeneutics must always be done from an ideological perspective. Though complete objectivity may be unattainable, the methods of biblical criticism do usually enable us to get closer to the original meaning of the text, and this is surely very important in determining its meaning and relevance for us today. 'Seeing' a text from an ideological point of view, moreover, can lead to distorting its meaning to support our own particular standpoint. An ideology is, after all, a personal preference which the holder believes is true. Whether it is in fact true will obviously be contested by people who cannot share it.

The ideological reading of Scripture, therefore, cannot provide us with a generally accepted principle for the understanding of the Bible in theology. In terms of our earlier definitions such approaches seem to confuse the task of exegesis (determining the meaning of the biblical text) with hermeneutics (interpreting that meaning for our own time). Another problem is that ideologies are never permanent. When an ideology is called into serious question (as has happened with Marxism following the collapse of Communism in Eastern Europe) its usefulness as a framework for theology becomes increasingly difficult.

THE LITERARY CATEGORY

Let us return to higher criticism. Its first task, we may remember, was to examine the literary category of a piece of writing. The Bible, of course, unlike Shakespeare's *Macbeth* or Ngugi's *The River Between*, is not a single work. It is a collection or library of literary works, and it therefore presents us with a great variation of literary forms. Our first step in using a particular biblical book, then, will be to determine what particular literary category the writer of that book is using.

A great deal of the Old Testament, for example, is poetry. The Psalms, Proverbs and Song of Songs are all poetical books, and there are a good many songs scattered throughout the narrative books. The Book of Job is a great poetic drama, and large sections of the prophetical writings are also cast in poetic form. A good translation of the Bible will show this clearly by the way it is set out. In the New Testament we have poems in the first two chapters of the Gospel of Luke, and snatches of early Christian hymns are preserved in some of the Epistles. It is also quite likely that some of Jesus' teaching was given in poetic form. These parts of the Bible need to be approached and interpreted as poetry, and full allowance will have to be made for the language and symbolism of the poetic imagination. But in the Bible the dividing line between poetry and prose is not very exact. Allegories (e.g. Ezek. 16 and 23, Isa. 5 and John 10.1–14) and parables both fall into the literary category of poetic story-telling. They are not literal narratives, but freely invented poetic stories which have a moral and religious point.

There are two other categories which closely resemble poetry and which are often misunderstood. The first of these is myth. We have already met this term in chapter 2 when we referred to Bultmann's attempt to 'demythologize' the New Testament. As used in literary criticism, 'myth' does not mean 'untrue' – as it usually does in popular speech. Rather it means a piece of poetic literature, often cast in story form, which is not meant so much to describe 'what happened' as to expose people's spiritual experience. In Genesis chapters 1 to 11, for example, the writer has reworked myths which were current in the ancient Middle East to make them vehicles of theological teaching – God as Creator, human beings as alienated from God by sin, the inevitability of judgement and so on. The importance of these stories does not lie in whether they happened or not, but in the description they give of the spiritual condition of men and women, of our existential situation. Ironically, the needless controversies between science and religion of an earlier century were at root less a misunderstanding of science than a misunderstanding of the real nature and purpose of these sections of Scripture.

The other semi-poetic form is 'apocalyptic'*, a term which comes from the Greek word meaning 'to reveal'. While there are only two apocalyptic books in the Bible – Daniel and Revelation – apocalyptic language is found in many parts of the Old Testament (especially the Prophets) and also in the Gospels and a few of the Epistles. Apocalyptic is a very specialized style of writing, which usually originates from people suffering oppression and persecution. It uses a kind of secret language of symbols and images, often strange and bizarre, and is meant to convey a message of hope and ultimate triumph of good over evil. To take such language literally is quite to miss the point the writer is making.

Much of the Bible is often read as history, but it is important to recognize that history as a literary category does not exist in the Bible. The 'historical'* books of the Old Testament (Joshua-Judges, Samuel, Kings) are classified in the Hebrew Bible as 'Prophets', that is, they were understood not in the modern sense of history as 'facts', but rather as the proclamation of God's power through events. Consequently the Old Testament writers were less interested in facts and figures (which is a very modern way of looking at the past), than in interpreting history as a witness to the acts of God for salvation. The same may be said of the Gospels. Indeed the earliest gospel-writer, Mark, found that there was no literary category in existence which exactly suited his purpose, and invented the new category 'gospel', or proclamation of good news. Looked at from this point of view many of the historical problems which arise from time to time in our study of the Bible do not appear very significant. The essence of biblical authority is located not in historical accuracy but in religious proclamation.

The second task of higher criticism can be more briefly dealt with. Primarily this seeks to determine the time of the writing. The point of this is to place the text firmly within its historical, cultural and sociopolitical context. Our understanding of the Book of Amos, for example, will be very slight if we do not appreciate that he was preaching against a background of political instability and social fragmentation during the eighth century BC in the northern kingdom of Israel. At that time the ruling classes were living extravagantly at the expense of the poor, whose lands and liberties were being violated. We shall further understand Amos' reaction to this situation when we appreciate his own origins (Amos 7.14ff). Again, Isaiah 40—55 is incomprehensible except within the context of the imminent release of the exiles from Babylon and their return to their own land. In the New Testament Paul's letters to the Corinthian Church presuppose a series of problems between him and some of the Corinthian Christians, as well as serious problems within the Church itself. The Epistles of John deal with a group which seems to have denied the true human nature of Jesus. We could multiply examples.

Our point is that each biblical book presupposes a particular time and situation – the biblical books are all 'situational' or 'occasional'. To appreciate what that background or occasion of writing was will open up the deeper level of the meaning of the text. The task of discovering this background and context may indeed sometimes be a very hard one. Many parts of the Bible (especially the Pentateuch and Prophets) have undergone a long process of editing and expansion. In others the writers used ancient traditions (often oral) which they reworked to suit their own purposes. Furthermore all the biblical writers had their own viewpoints, which determined to some extent the use they made of their raw materials. Sometimes these viewpoints – what we might call the philosophy of the writer – are made quite explicit (for example in 2 Kings 17.7–18 or John 20.30–31). More often they are implied.

All these aspects of the biblical text – time of writing, situation, aims of the author – will have to be taken into account before a passage of the Bible can be confidently used in doing Christian theology.

THE ACCURACY OF THE BIBLICAL TEXT

We have seen that the actual text of the Bible is sometimes in doubt. It is important, as far as possible, to make sure that the text we are using is authentic, that is, the text that the author himself actually wrote. This is the task of textual criticism. Textual critics examine in detail the various extant versions of the Hebrew and Greek text of the Bible, as well as ancient translations and biblical quotations in early Christian writings, and by a process of meticulous comparison and the application of certain basic principles, come to reasonable conclusions as to what the original text is likely to have been. Such a task clearly involves considerable linguistic and scholarly expertise, which is usually beyond the capacity (or indeed the time) of the normal doers of theology. They will usually be content to use the labours of the textual critics.

Theologians with little knowledge of Greek and Hebrew will obviously be at a grave disadvantage here. Not only will they be unable to appreciate the subtle emphases of the original text, but they may also miss out on the important overtones of key words (e.g. *shalom** (peace), *hesed** (mercy), *agape** (love), *pistis** (faith)) where the English words used in translation do not carry the depth and variety of meaning of the original Hebrew or Greek. There is therefore a very strong case for anyone who aspires to do theology in any depth to acquire at least a working knowledge of biblical languages. Aids such as lexicons, dictionaries and critical commentaries, which discuss the meaning of individual words and the structure of the text, are essential.

Theologians who depend largely upon translations are at the disadvantage of being one stage removed from their sources. If this has to be the case, then it is essential to use a translation which aims as far as possible to get at the literal meaning of the text. The Revised Standard Version (though it sounds a little awkward in places) has the advantage of keeping fairly close to the original Greek and Hebrew, and gives alternative translations and the readings of different important manuscripts at the foot of the page. Comparing several translations of the same passage is often also helpful, though it needs to be kept in mind that some of the more popular modern versions (such as the Good News Bible) are not really translations so much as free interpretations, and sometimes stray away from the literal meaning of the original.

The first stage of using the Bible in Christian theology, then, is a careful examination of the literary category and authorship of the text, and of its historical, cultural and socio-political background, with a view to determining its meaning for the people of its own time. The second task is the hermeneutical one: how does the Bible, which speaks directly only to the men and women of its own time, speak to us today, and how do we use it to create a theology which will answer to our own needs?

USING THE BIBLE IN DOING THEOLOGY

None of the biblical books sets out to be a textbook on systematic theology. Each reflects a different and particular situation in the life of the people of God. Theologians also address a specific situation within the life of the Church. Their task is to transfer the essence of the message of each biblical book from its own time to their time. They therefore seek to bridge the 'hermeneutical gap' between the situation of the original hearers of the word of God and their own situation. This task we will address more fully in chapters 5 and 6, but at this point a few broad principles can be suggested.

First, it is likely that some parts of the Bible will be more relevant to the theologians' situation than others. Which parts they emphasize and which parts they neglect will depend upon many factors, not least which books of the Bible appear to them to be closer to their own situation. In the history of theology it is clear enough that some biblical books have had an influence far in excess of others. The Epistle to the Romans, for example, played a dominant role in the theology of Augustine, of Luther and, in more recent times, of Karl Barth. Through these figures it has shaped a good deal of Western theology.

It is probably reasonable to expect that the New Testament will have more influence on Christian theology than the Old, though this is not always the case, and in Africa some important sections of the Church seem to show a special interest in the legal parts of the Old Testament and in those 'Hebraic' portions of the New, like James and Hebrews. Some Asian theologians, on the other hand, have felt more affinity with the reflective philosophical approach of the Johannine writings. There is indeed a real danger that selectivity may lead to distortion and overemphasis upon one aspect of the Gospel.

For this reason a second principle is that the theologians should, as far as possible, be comprehensive in their use of Scripture, that is, they should draw insights from different parts of the Bible and compare them to gain a holistic and well-rounded view. In seeking to expound the meaning of the death of Christ, for example, the predominantly narrative portions of the Gospels will need to be understood and interpreted in the light of the teaching of Jesus Himself about His death, and in the light of the sacrificial and legal symbolism used by Paul, John,

1 Peter, and in Hebrews. Each of these writers looks at and interprets the crucifixion from a somewhat different perspective; and each perspective ought to be taken into account in arriving at a theology of the atonement. This should not involve forcing meanings upon texts arbitrarily – interpreting Paul in the light of John, for example, or vice versa. Theologians, therefore, need to recognize the freedom of the individual author, while at the same time seeking a complete understanding of a particular doctrine. The biblical authority for this doctrine will in this way be soundly based in the whole of the Scripture rather than on isolated (and perhaps imperfectly understood) 'prooftexts'.

The final and difficult task is to relate the message of the biblical writers to the context of the person actually doing theology. This process has variously been described as one of 'contextualization'*, 'indigenization'* and 'adaptationism'* (or 'adaptionism'). We shall return to this issue in chapter 5.

STUDY SUGGESTIONS

WORDS AND MEANINGS
1. What do you understand by the following terms when applied to the Bible?
   (a) authoritative;
   (b) inspired;
   (c) Word of God.
2. Define briefly:
   (a) higher criticism;
   (b) contextual criticism.
3. In higher criticism, what is the difference between exegesis and hermeneutics?
4. Explain what is meant by:
   (a) literary categories;
   (b) hermeneutical gap;
   (c) apocalyptic;
   and give an example of each.

REVIEW OF CONTENT
5. What two principles does the writer of this book suggest are essential for an understanding of a passage from the Bible?
6. Why do we need to understand the historical and cultural background in interpreting a passage from the Bible?
7. What is meant by 'ideological' readings of Scripture, and what are their advantages and disadvantages?

8 What is the 'fundamentalist' view of the Bible, and what problems does it raise?

CONTEXTUAL APPLICATION AND DISCUSSION

9 'The Bible does not speak to our present situation as though the two thousand years in between did not exist' (p. 24). What do you consider the most important ways in which our present situation differs from the situations when the different books of the Bible were written? And what are the consequent implications for our understanding of the Bible today?
10 'The authority of the Bible is not located in historical accuracy but in religious proclamation' (p. 30). Do you agree? Give your reasons.
11 Why is it that some books of the Bible have had more influence on Christian thought than others? Which particular books do you think are the most important for Christians in your own country today, and why?
12 Some Christians claim that the New Testament presents us with a variety of theologies from different authors, and ask if there is any advantage in seeking a well-rounded and 'holistic' view of Scripture. What is your opinion? Give your reasons.

4

The History of Theology

THE IMPORTANCE OF THE HISTORY OF CHRISTIAN THOUGHT

We saw in chapter 3 that the Bible is the foundation document of Christian theology and its primary 'objective' source. We also noted that our knowledge of God can never be completely separated from our human response to Him. In this sense theology is essentially the verbalization of His revelation to us as His creatures. Theology, therefore, involves taking seriously the way in which Christians throughout the centuries have known and experienced Him, that is, it involves the study of the human response to God in the history of the Christian Church. We then need to evaluate these interpretations in the light of our own experience of God. Thus church history, and especially the formulation by the Church of doctrine, provides us with additional sources for doing theology.

It is, of course, possible to argue that after about AD 120 (that is, after the last New Testament book had been written) the Church fell into error and quite misunderstood the meaning of the Gospel, and therefore the only way to do theology is to go 'back to the Bible'. This is indeed a position which some Christians would support. But it seems rather a drastic stance, and it would in any case still be necessary, if one held this view, to study the sources of Christian thought after AD 120 in order to explain exactly how the Church did get it all wrong. And if the faith became tainted, how are we able to know that our own present perspective is not also in error?

Probably most Christians would not want to be so dismissive of 2,000 years of Christian history. And in practice a good deal of theology contains a large amount of dialogue with the past and seeks to enter into debate with Christian thinkers of earlier generations. This does not mean that all of Christian tradition, or indeed all received doctrine, is necessarily correct or even relevant, nor does it mean that we have to accept uncritically the statements of Christian faith that have been generally accepted by the Church as a whole. But at the same time we should remember that certain statements of faith – like the ecumenical creeds – and great theologians of the past – like Augustine, Aquinas, Luther and Calvin – have had an enormous influence upon the thinking of the Church. It seems only sensible, therefore, to take their contributions seriously when doing theology.

It is usually assumed that certain periods in the history of the Church are more important for the study of theology than others. In a sense the periods which are regarded as critical to an understanding of the Christian faith will depend to some extent on the section of the Church to which we belong. Catholic theologians will probably lay more emphasis on the pre-Reformation period, while most Protestants would concentrate on the Reformation* itself.

To some degree our choice of the periods which we regard as the most important will be rather arbitrary. But careful theologians will try to guard against being too selective. They will try, as far as possible, to understand positions which they cannot feel much sympathy for. To do this they will have to explore periods in the history of doctrine which are of limited interest to them. At the same time, a comprehensive grasp of the whole history of doctrine is essential for putting each new development in its context. It would be misleading, for example, to begin a study of the Reformation at 1517 without going back to find out what it was that prompted Luther's protest, or to study Karl Barth's theology without understanding just what he was reacting against. But having said that, life is clearly too short to study all periods in the history of theology in the same detail, and in practice some degree of specialization will be necessary.

FORMATION OF THE CANON

Most Christians of all traditions would agree that the first four or five hundred years of Christianity were especially important, for these early centuries were a formative period for the Church in many ways. It was during these years, for example, that the Christian Church considered its attitude to the Bible as the main source of its authority. It would not be completely correct, though, to claim that the early church Fathers defined the way in which the Bible constituted divine revelation. There were divergent approaches to this issue, and in particular a difference between the more literal school of Antioch and the more allegorical* approach of the Alexandrians. But in another important respect the early Church did have to define the boundaries of what was to be regarded as the word of God or the 'canon' of Scripture – which books should be contained in the Bible and which excluded.

As far as the Old Testament is concerned, the Palestinian Church by and large took over the books which the Jews of Palestine regarded as authoritative (though the Jewish rabbis in Palestine did not come to any formal agreement about their own canon until very much later). Hellenistic* Jews, that is, those Jews who spoke Greek and in general lived outside Palestine, were rather more liberal in their approach to Scripture and accepted in addition as inspired those books which are now known by Protestant Christians as the Apocrypha and by Catholics as the Deutero-canonical Books. These were included in the Greek translation of the Old Testament, which is known as the Septuagint* (for which the symbol LXX is usually used). This translation was begun about the third century BC, though not fully completed until much later. It was necessary because many Jews living outside Palestine (the 'diaspora'* or 'dispersed') had lost the ability to read the Old Testament fluently in Hebrew and habitually used only Greek.

The question of the New Testament is rather more complicated. Most New Testament books seem to have been accepted as authoritative fairly early on, probably on the grounds that they had some degree of apostolic authority (though we know now that this is disputed, to one degree or another, of all four Gospels!). Some shorter books, like Philemon, 2 and 3 John, 2 Peter and Jude (the last two of very doubtful apostolic authorship) were disputed until quite late, as also was the Book of Revelation. The earliest complete list of the canonical New Testament books was not drawn up until the Council of Carthage in AD 337.

As is well known, Luther had little regard for the Epistle of James which, along with Hebrews, he relegated to a secondary position. In this he was followed by some of the other Reformers. At the same time other Christian books not now included in the Bible, such as the *Shepherd of Hermas* and the *Didache*, were very highly regarded by many of the earliest Christians. The exact cut-off point at which books were accepted as canonical is therefore a little arbitrary. Today most theologians would probably recognize the particular value of those books which the early Church in its wisdom declared as canonical and authoritative, but at the same time many would argue that some of the other Christian writings from the first and second centuries are also very useful in the task of doing theology.

LITURGY AND CREEDS

Another important way in which the early centuries of Christianity became normative for the Church was in the development of liturgy and church structures. Christian liturgy was originally to quite a large degree derived from the worship of the Jewish synagogue, with its pattern of singing of psalms, readings from Scripture (usually two, one from the Torah*, a second from the Prophets) and an exposition in the vernacular. In time, as the Church increasingly broke free from its Jewish roots, both its worship and organization evolved in new directions. But much of what is generally accepted today owes its origins to the early centuries. Liturgy and worship are also raw materials for the task of doing theology (see chapter 1).

The most important achievement of the early Church as far as Christian theology is concerned, however, lies undoubtedly in its statements of doctrine, both through the writings of the church Fathers and especially in the pronouncements of the great creeds which are still accepted by large sections of the Church today. Christian doctrine in the early centuries was essentially thrashed out in the context of controversy. This led to acceptance of the view that some teaching is 'orthodox'*, ('right', 'correct') and other teaching is false ('heterodox' or 'heresy'*). It is important to understand, however, that the terms 'dogma'* and 'heresy' both derive from Greek words which simply imply a personal opinion. 'Dogma' is related to the impersonal verb *dokei moi** which means 'it seems to me'. Only later does 'dogma' come to harden into the meaning which it has today of 'an organized presentation of the truth about Christianity'. 'Heresy' actually means 'choice' and is used in that sense in the New Testament itself (it is also used of a religious 'party', such as the Pharisees). Again the development of this word to the derogatory meaning of 'false teaching' came later.

These changes in meaning indicate how the mind of the Church developed over the first few centuries. The Christian faith came to be seen as a body of doctrine: certain 'true' statements about the nature of God and Christ which could – and indeed if one wanted to remain within the 'orthodox' Church had to – be assented to. Indeed the fact that the creeds were felt to be necessary at all shows us very clearly that the early Church was not at all agreed about matters of belief.

It has been suggested that the introduction of creeds has not been altogether a wholesome development, since it tends to present Christianity as putting more emphasis upon intellectual assent rather than on personal commitment. For this reason many theologians, especially in the Third World, would argue that what we need now is not so much orthodoxy (right belief) as orthopraxis* (right action).

We shall perhaps understand better what the creeds are meant to accomplish if we put them in their historical context. The Apostolic Fathers* were, in the main, sufficiently influenced by hellenism (Greek thought and culture) to believe that religious truth could be reduced to a system and could be defined exactly by the use of the right terms. The creeds therefore are, in a sense, an exercise in inculturation*, that is, they clothed ideas, which originated in the Jewish Palestinian world, in the language of the non-Jewish-speaking Christians who very soon came to make up the great majority of the Church.

There was an immediate problem here. Put very broadly, the Jewish concept of God, derived from the Old Testament, was a dynamic one of a God who is actively involved in historical events for the salvation of His people. The Greek approach, largely derived from the philosophy of

Plato, was more timeless – God is absolute and changeless perfection, transcendent* rather than immanent*. It is not at all easy to combine these two different perceptions. Now while it is true, of course, that the creeds make statements about the 'events' of the Gospel – the incarnation, the crucifixion, the resurrection – the first of these (and the most fundamental, for the others logically depend upon it) is defined in the longer creeds in terms which are very remote indeed from the language of the New Testament itself. If we are rightly to understand the creeds and to make use of them in doing theology we shall therefore have to take seriously into account their use of Greek philosophy. This was not part of the experience of the earliest Christians and is also very remote from the experience of most Christians today.

Just as in understanding the Bible we have to ask what it meant to the original hearers, so we have to do the same thing with the creeds. Indeed this task is probably even more crucial, for we are faced in the creeds with statements which sound very strange to modern ears – 'God from God', 'of the same substance with the Father', 'begotten not made' and so on. If we are to grasp the intentions of the Christians who coined such phrases, we shall have to know why they felt it necessary to express their faith in this way.

At this point the names which have been attached to the three great ecumenical creeds do not help us very much. The Apostles' Creed, for instance, is certainly not the work of the Apostles. Though its origins probably go back to the second century, in its present form it is several centuries later than that, and in fact was only really accepted in the Western Church. The Nicene Creed was not the statement of faith agreed at the Council of Nicaea in AD 325, but came from the later Council of Constantinople. And the Athanasian Creed has very little to do with Athanasius! It is probably a document from the fifth century intended originally to be used in catechetical* teaching.

But, on the other hand, some of the terminology reflected in these creeds does reflect the controversies of the earlier periods. Some of these controversies were not very much to the credit of the Church, and reveal a good deal of personal animosity and back-door politics. But the orthodox Christians did genuinely believe that they were defining the biblical faith in what to them were modern ways, and we must assume that, in general, it was their passion for what they believed to be the truth which led to their readiness to 'anathematize'* and hence exclude those who did not agree with them. The intention of the creeds was to try to define explicitly what (so it was assumed) was believed implicitly by all good Christians. In one sense, therefore, the creeds draw parameters or boundaries, outside of which (so it was thought) it was not possible to stray and still remain Christian.

In the event large sections of the Church did, from time to time, object to some phrase or other in the statements of faith which seemed to them to be going beyond what they felt could legitimately be said, and they suffered exclusion or withdrew from the Catholics (the 'universal, world-wide Church'). In the fifth century, for example, the followers of Nestorius, a Bishop of Constantinople, objected to the description of Mary as *theotokos** or 'bearer of God' because they wanted a clearer distinction between the human and the divine natures of Christ. The main body of the Church accepted the title as expressing the ground of the unity of Christ's person, human and divine; the Nestorians were excluded. However, they spread eastwards, outside the Roman Empire, and eventually reached as far as China.

The bigger schism some hundreds of years later, was between the Eastern ('Orthodox') and the Western ('Catholic') Churches. One factor in this split (along with a good deal of ecclesiastical politics) was the objection by the Orthodox to the insertion by the Western Church of the phrase 'and the Son' in the article in the Nicene Creed concerning the Spirit. (The original text read: 'I believe in the Holy Spirit, the Lord, the Giver of Life, who proceeds from the Father.')

INTERPRETING THE CREEDS

How should we make use of the ecumenical creeds when doing theology? Most theologians would regard them not so much as definitions but as guidelines to a correct expression or verbalization of the Christian faith. On this view we do not so much need to accept the terminology or the thought-forms of the creeds (which are in the main quite foreign to our experience today), but much more the fundamental ideas which they are meant to convey. Thus in our own age and context we shall probably have to look for other ways to describe the uniqueness of Jesus rather than merely to repeat that He is 'of one substance with the Father' or 'begotten not made'. The essence of these statements is to preserve the real humanity and real divinity of Jesus. Our task will be to explore these realities in terms which fit our modern cultures, just as the creeds fitted the hellenized cultures of the first few centuries of the Christian era. In this sense it would not be a bad thing to attempt to rewrite the creeds in terms of our own cultures, philosophies and religious context – though such an exercise would probably cause the same kind of controversy as that which surrounded the Councils of Nicaea and Chalcedon!

In understanding the creeds we shall also need to recognize not only that they (like the Bible) use language which is historically and culturally conditioned, but also that some of this language is symbolic: it can be understood on more than one level. Let us take the apparently simple statement: 'He ascended into heaven'. This may be understood on a purely literal level, as the early Christians probably understood it and as medieval Christian art, with its portrayal of Jesus disappearing into the clouds, has accustomed us to visualize it.

But on reflection it is apparent that this is not a 'historical' statement in the same way as 'He was crucified'. The latter statement is historically verifiable (in so far as any event is historically verifiable). Statements like 'He ascended into heaven' are not verifiable in the same sense. They are statements of faith, not of fact, and can only really be made by those who believe that Jesus was more than simply a human figure. Such statements point beyond the literal meaning. 'He ascended into heaven' includes within it the idea that Jesus is no longer bound to earth (in the same sense that human beings usually are when they die), and that He somehow shares in the life of God in a new manner. In the same way 'He is seated at the right hand of God' is not a statement about the physical posture and location of Jesus, but an affirmation that He shares in God's rule and authority.

Many theologians would go further and argue that the literal meaning of these credal statements is relatively secondary and that what really matters is their significance for faith. Here we are back again at the problem which was raised in relation to religious language: where do we draw the line between what is meant literally and what is symbolical or metaphorical? It also raises another question which is of great importance to theology, the relationship between faith and history. (See chapter 7, p. 71.)

RELEVANCE OF THEOLOGICAL MOVEMENTS

In our consideration of the early Church we have concentrated so far on formal statements of Christian doctrine, since most Churches would regard at least the three great ecumenical creeds as, to one degree or another, binding upon Christians today. But there are also other lessons which can be learned from the early centuries with regard to doctrine, especially the way in which its formation was influenced by social and political interaction.

To give just two examples: the Montanist movement in the second century was an attempt to revive the freedom of the Holy Spirit in prophecy, and the course of its history is not without relevance to an evaluation of the charismatic* movement and to church ministry in our own time. Donatism, which arose some two centuries later and became dominant in North Africa, began as a bid to preserve purity in the Church, but subsequently developed into a protest movement of the peasant poor, who rejected the jurisdiction of the state in the affairs of the Church. These are issues of crucial importance in some Third World countries today. A study of church history, and especially the history of doctrine, may therefore help to point the way forward to contemporary Christian problems.

LATER STATEMENTS OF FAITH

Although most Churches accept one or more of the creeds, many of them tend to go beyond these primary statements of faith and also have their own confessions or creeds, which are binding on their adherents. The Roman Catholic Church regards its traditions, especially those enshrined in papal decrees, as authoritative. In our own time the Second Vatican Council (Vatican II*, 1962–5) has provided a great impetus to Catholic theology, both in freeing Catholic thinkers from some of the restrictions of the past and in opening up new avenues for theological exploration in the world-wide context.

Non-Catholic Churches, too, have their confessions, which were often worked out in conflict with Catholicism. Such are, for example, the Augsburg Confession of the Lutheran Churches (1530), the Thirty-Nine Articles of the Anglican Church (1662, based on the Forty-Two Articles of 1552), and the Westminster Confession of the Reformed Churches* (1642), to name only some of the most famous. All such confessions came out of particular unrepeatable historical contexts, but in time passed into the 'tradition' accepted by these various Churches.

Christian theologians, as we have noted, work from particular ecclesiastical traditions too – whether Catholic, Reformed, or other. Extending the metaphor we used earlier, we might regard particular traditions as smaller circles within the larger theological circle. All theologians, therefore, have as part of their task to make sense of the church tradition within which they stand, in its relation to the wider context of the Church as a whole and their own life contexts. There will almost certainly be times when they will be forced to question the correctness of aspects of their own tradition. There may indeed be times when their findings lead them to abandon their tradition for another which seems to them to be more in tune with the primary sources of the Christian faith or with their own experience of God.

In this sense, then, theologians both choose their theological tradition and at the same time also question it. The essential thing is that they are able to exercise freedom in relating what they learn from their church tradition to what they learn from the Bible, Christian history and their own spirituality.

THE AUTHORITY OF THE CHURCH

At this point we are faced with the important question of just what kind of authority the Church has for theology. Some Churches are authoritarian. For Roman Catholics, for example, it is the Church which decrees within fairly strict parameters, what is to be believed. The Protestant reaction to this position at the time of the Reformation was twofold – the Reformers emphasized the authority of Scripture on the one hand, and the individual conscience on the other. But in practice today some Reformed Churches may also restrict the freedom of their theologians quite severely on what are regarded as essential Christian doctrines.

There is no easy answer to the problem of external authority (the Church) versus subjective authority (the individual conscience). Even the *sola scriptura** ('by Scripture alone') of the Reformers did not solve this problem, for it simply threw it back to the issue of whose interpretation of Scripture – the Church's or the individual's – was to be preferred. In the last analysis theology is an individual activity which, at the same time, has to be carried out within the context of a church community if it is to have any real meaning, and which necessarily also reflects that community's experience of God.

THE IMPACT OF WESTERN PHILOSOPHY AND SCIENCE ON THEOLOGY

The emphasis upon the role of the individual, though in a large degree originating from the Reformation, received great impetus from the stress upon reason which marked the period in Western thought known as the Enlightenment*. This stress on reason was in turn questioned by such philosophers as Immanuel Kant (1724–1804) and David Hume (1711–76). Kant was a German thinker, who had an immense influence on Christian theology when he developed the view that truth and value are not to be found in the being of God but rather in what he called the 'transcendental' dimension of the human spirit. In Britain, Hume founded the movement known as Empiricism*. Empiricism in its turn gave birth to the scientific method and the historical method, both of which also had important consequences for theology. The former stressed the role of sense data* (that is, what could be verified from our physical senses) and empirical observation as a means of arriving at truth. This approach (aided by the publication in 1859 of Charles Darwin's *The Origin of Species*) called in question those beliefs of Christianity – such as the doctrine of creation, the virgin birth, the resurrection, miracles and so on – which could not be scientifically proved on the basis of sense data.

The historical method, which also owed a lot to the writings of the German philosopher Hegel (1770–1831) led directly to the historical-critical approach to the Bible and to the belief that it had to be examined just like any other ancient book. The impact of scientific and historical methods on Christian theology has been dramatic. Some more conservative Christians have largely ignored the impact of these methods, but such an approach cannot help us very much to relate Christian faith to the world as it is today. The task of modern theology is to address those problems with which advances in philosophical and scientific knowledge confront us.

THE IMPORTANCE OF THIRD WORLD THEOLOGY

Just as the eighteenth and nineteenth centuries saw a dramatic expansion of the Christian faith into the non-Western world, so the twentieth century witnessed an equally dramatic development in Christian theology in those continents. Unfortunately, too many Western theologians appear to be unaware of the phenomenon of 'Third World Theology'. On the other hand, contact between theologians from Latin America, Africa and Asia has increased remarkably over the last few decades, and there is increasing evidence of cross-fertilization of theological insights from one continent to another.

Probably the best known of Third World theologies has been the theology of liberation, which came out of Latin America during the 1960s, and which focused especially on the importance of social and economic factors in seeing theology as the active liberation of the poor and oppressed in all areas of life, material as well as spiritual. In its methodology* the theology of liberation was very much indebted to an analysis of society based on the thinking of Karl Marx, and it is closer to Western models than are many African and Asian theologies.

In Asia (except for the Philippines) Christianity is very much a minority religion (only about 3% overall), and the Church has therefore had to pay special attention to other ancient religions and their relationship to the Christian faith. Indian Christian theology has a long history, as befits a country which claims a Christian tradition going back to the apostolic age. By the first half of the nineteenth century Indian Christians had already begun to think out their faith in relation to Hinduism, and in the twentieth century they broadened their concerns to take in issues of society, class and caste.

The theologies which have emerged from Africa since the 1960s have been especially concerned with relating the Christian faith to African cultures and with what has been called 'anthropological poverty' – the cultural as well as the material loss which has been brought about by the colonial domination of Africa by the West. In South Africa Black theology has stressed the dignity of black identity in a situation in which Africans were marginalized and oppressed by a ruling white minority. We shall refer, by way of illustration, to some of these exciting developments in modern theology in the remaining chapters of this book.

From what has been said it should be evident that doctrine or 'dogma' is not something static that has been given once for all and that never changes. On the contrary, Christian doctrine – theology – is dynamic and ever-developing as it seeks to meet the new challenges with which it is brought face to face in a changing modern world. In reformulating theology to each new situation, the Bible, the history of the Church and of Christian thought, the traditions and institutions of the Churches, and the inner experiences of individual believers, all have their part to play.

STUDY SUGGESTIONS

WORDS AND MEANINGS

1 Briefly define each of the following:
   (a) canon of Scripture;
   (b) Apocrypha or Deutero-canonical Writings;
   (c) the Septuagint.
2 Explain what is meant by:
   (a) hellenistic Jews;
   (b) a smaller circle within the larger theological circle;
   (c) anthropological poverty.

REVIEW OF CONTENT

3 Why is it impossible to ignore 2,000 years of Christian history when we do theology?
4 For what chief reasons are the first 500 years of the Church regarded as especially important?
5 What are the circumstances and criteria which led to the canon of Scripture being defined?
6 What are the main differences between the Judaeo-Christian and the Greek Christian approaches to theology?
7 What challenges to theology were presented by the work of each of the following:
   (a) Kant;
   (b) Hume;
   (c) Darwin;
   (d) Hegel?
8 What new challenges and questions have arisen from the development of Christian theology in:
   (a) Asia;
   (b) Africa, and
   (c) Latin America?

CONTEXTUAL APPLICATION AND DISCUSSION

9 What criteria would you use in deciding which periods of church history are most important for doing theology today, and why?
10 Do you consider that creeds are necessary? If so, for what chief purpose or purposes?
11 Examine the statements of faith used by your own Church. How far are they:
   (a) the product of a particular historical and cultural context;
   (b) still relevant to the present-day situation;
   (c) understandable by ordinary Christians in your country?
12 Have any translations of the Christian creeds into the languages of your country been adapted to suit the culture and context of the area? If not, experiment in rewriting the Apostles' Creed to suit the context of your own Church.
13 How do you think the Montanist and Donatist movements can help in understanding your Church situation today? What other movements in the early Church have their parallel in the Church today?

5

Taking Account of Culture

THE IMPORTANCE OF CULTURE TO DOING THEOLOGY

In the last two chapters we looked at the Bible and Christian tradition, the raw materials which theologians have to hand when they seek to think creatively about God. While our understanding of the Bible may, and hopefully does, become greater as time goes on, and while the understanding of the Church with regard to the cardinal aspects of doctrine is constantly developing, these are both sources of theology whose 'deposit' is constant. They may therefore be regarded as the foundation materials of any theology which claims the name Christian. But these foundational materials are never understood in a vacuum. They always come to the believer within a particular context.

This context itself is constantly changing. For the earliest Christians it was the context of Palestinian Judaism and the hellenistic world. For the Protestant Reformers it was the world of late medievalism. For Christians in the Third World today it is the context of modern Asia, Africa, Oceania, Latin America and the Caribbean. It is the context within which the source materials are perceived which gives to Christianity its relevance, and each one of us has such a context or framework from which we understand our Christian faith.

That context is determined by many things: by our national and racial heritage, for example, by our place within a given society, by our education and upbringing, by our personal experience of the world. The context or framework within which we understand the Gospel will obviously differ from person to person and from country to country. A middle-class German is unlikely to bring to his theological insights the same experiences as a Brazilian peasant. An Indian Christian living as an adherent of a minority religion among his Hindu and Muslim compatriots will have different perceptions from a South American Catholic living in a largely Christianized continent. An African believer living under a military dictatorship or one-party state will probably experience God rather differently from one living in a Western democracy.

These are all factors which affect how we live and feel, and they will also affect the way we think about God. To understand the framework within which any particular theologian (or indeed any Christian) does his or her work is to go a long way towards a sympathetic appreciation of his or her exposition of the Christian faith, and thereby to enrich our own theological understanding. Every theology has its own particular and individual qualities, whether its practitioners openly acknowledge this or not. These particular qualities have many elements which interact with one another and which are important determinants of the way people express their faith. In the following pages we shall look more closely at some of these broad contexts or frameworks within which theology is done, drawing our illustrations as far as possible from theology in the non-Western world. The first of these is culture.

CULTURE: A DEFINITION

The *Concise Oxford Dictionary* defines culture as 'intellectual development'. While it certainly includes this, such a definition is very restricted. The pioneer anthropologist Malinowski suggested a wider definition, which is more useful for our purposes. For him culture included inherited artefacts, goods, technical processes, ideas, habits and values. This is much more comprehensive. On this definition culture has three main aspects: the material, the ethical and the intellectual.

Cultures are formed partly by the technologies they use to sustain life: that is, by the methods used to obtain food (whether hunting, gathering or planting), by housing structures, by tools, and so on. They are also determined by behaviour patterns, relationships within the family, clan or wider community of outsiders. Especially important here is the cohesion of the family as a whole and the rituals which are employed to cement that cohesion. Behaviour patterns in respect to the environment are also important, particularly in predominantly rural groups. Finally, culture is shaped by ideas – concepts of God, the supernatural world, right and wrong, the nature and destiny of mankind, and so on. These ideas are often expressed in oral literature and acted out in rituals.

While these three aspects of culture – the material, the ethical and the intellectual – can be distinguished for the purposes of definition, they are not mutually exclusive and they closely interact with one another. Religious ideas, especially, may affect not only personal relationships but also attitudes towards the environment and food production. Culture is therefore all-embracing.

It is also essentially defined within the group. It is communal and the forms it takes often provide outsiders with a means of recognizing the essential characteristics of the group. Culture never exists in the abstract – it is always somebody's culture. Thus we may speak of Aztec culture, or of Akan culture or, more broadly, of Western culture. By this we mean the accumulation of technology and science, morals and behaviour, ideas and values, which characterize that particular section of the human race, their 'world-view' (for which the German term *Weltanschauung** is often used).

Cultures are in a sense limiting, for they act as markers, marking one group off from another. Small-scale societies have cultures which are often fairly straightforward and which usually have a very strong hold over the behaviour of their members, for the worst punishment of all is to be excluded from the group. Even in large-scale societies, in India or China, for example, conformity to social custom is often highly regarded.

THREE CHARACTERISTICS OF CULTURE

Broadly speaking, cultures are marked by three characteristics: firstly, they are *inherited*, secondly, they *undergo change and modification*, and thirdly, they are *transmitted*. Cultures are inherited in as much as their technologies, values and ideas are passed down from one generation to the next. Each one of us stands within a genealogy, a line of descent from our ancestors, and has inherited from them certain cultural forms and values. Though we may choose to react against this inherited culture, we cannot escape from it, for it will always remain part of our experience.

But cultures are not static. As culture contact, that is, the interaction of one culture with another, takes place and as knowledge within a culture develops, new views and new ideas take shape. As a result new forms of culture come into being and are added to, or perhaps replace, the deposit of the original culture. This modified culture is then passed on to the next generation. This process is true, to one degree or another, even of the most isolated cultures.

Culture, then, is dynamic and subject to change. Change may come to a culture from within as well as from outside. All cultures have innovators, whether we know their names or not, who may invent new techniques (like tools and machinery) and discover new sources of energy, or may originate new concepts and ideas. Most changes in culture – and often the most dramatic changes – come from outside, as people of different cultures come into contact with one another and exchange new skills and ideas. Such interaction of cultures existed even in the most remote societies, for no society is an island to itself.

The period of Western colonial expansion, beginning with the voyages of discovery in the fifteenth century and culminating in the modern age, greatly increased the rate of social and cultural change. In the colonial era the ideas and attitudes of Western cultures were exported to the colonized continents, causing a wide-ranging dislocation of non-Western cultures, societies and economies. Indeed some of the smaller cultural groups, like the Australian Aborigines and some American Indians, were all but wiped out, and even the most developed societies in Asia and Africa were significantly changed by the traumatic and aggressive impact of the Western world upon them. By contrast other aspects of traditional cultures, especially those associated with religion, often 'went underground' or sometimes provided rallying points for resistance to the new domination by the Europeans.

When two cultures clash the usual result is some kind of accommodation by society at large to the stronger culture. On an individual level, however, it may often bring about serious personal conflict, a kind of cultural schizophrenia* within the individual whose traditional way of life and values are suddenly and often brutally disrupted. Within the present century urbanization and rapid industrialization have greatly increased the interaction between peoples of different ethnic groups (often citizens of the same newly independent nation) and have been important further catalysts to rapid social and cultural change.

The wholesale disruption of non-Western cultures by the Western colonial expansion provoked in many countries a strong reaction which sought to preserve and revive the values of the traditional culture. The great intellectual and spiritual awakening which began in Bengal during the nineteenth century, associated with such figures as Keshav Chandra Sen, Ramakrishna and Vivekananda, is one example of an attempt to revive Hindu spiritual values in reaction to colonialism and Christianity. Mahatma Gandhi and Nehru also drew deeply on the roots of Indian culture, although in very different ways, in their struggle for political independence.

Africa asserted its cultural values during the independence movements of the 1950s and 1960s. Nkrumah's concept of 'African Personality' and Senghor's Négritude* are perhaps the best examples, but the socialist philosophies of Kaunda and Nyerere also claimed, in part, to be based upon a rediscovery of Africa's cultural past. In each case the emphasis was on the affirmation of identity, rooted in a past heritage but refined to suit a new context.

What has been said above is not meant to imply any value judgement on whether a culture is 'good' or 'bad'. A given culture tends to evolve to suit the society in which it exists, and it will inevitably include some undesirable as well as desirable elements. One common problem (and it is a fault to which Europeans are all too susceptible) is the tendency to condemn other cultures simply because they are different from our own, or (in the case of many Christians) to confuse Western culture with the essence of Christianity. It needs to be recognized that each of us looks at the world from the perspective of our own inherited culture, and we must be careful not to assume that our culture is necessarily the best for all human societies.

Indeed it can be argued that all cultures are, in a sense, God-given and are (as Tillich once put it) 'the coming together of the human and the divine'. Tillich concluded from this that one of the tasks of theology was to analyse carefully all aspects of human culture – its philosophy, literature, art and so on – and that such an analysis would reveal the human problems with which that culture was deeply concerned. For him the role of theology was to point to the answers to those questions in the Christian Gospel. So an investigation of culture was a preliminary task to the work of actually doing theology.

Cultural differences are a fact of the world in which we live. At the same time many societies are becoming more and more 'culturally mixed' as they draw upon and absorb different ethnic traditions and ideas. This may result, as Kwesi Dickson has pointed out, in some confusion over just what 'traditional culture' really is.

CULTURE AND THEOLOGY

What has all this to do with doing theology? Primarily, as we have just noted, it means recognizing that each one of us approaches the task of doing theology from within our own cultural heritage. However much we may live in and share sympathetically in the cultures of others, we cannot escape completely from that heritage. So we shall express our understanding of God and the world in the language and thought-forms of the cultural tradition in which we have been nurtured.

One of the justifiable criticisms of Christian missions has been that they tended to remove converts from their own societies and thereby cut them off from their cultural roots. As a result Christianity itself has often appeared foreign, and Christ as a figure alien to the way of life of the people. In some instances this procedure did perhaps succeed in cutting off converts from their cultural roots, but in many more cases it resulted in a sense of schizophrenia, in a divided loyalty between the old religious culture and the newly adopted Christian faith.

In order to attempt to overcome this sense of alienation, Christian theology in many African and Asian countries today is seeking to make use of cultural forms and symbols. This has variously been termed 'contextualization', 'adaptionism' (or adaptationism) and 'indigenization'. Though these terms have slightly different emphases, their overall aim is to express the Christian faith in terms which each society can relate to and to clothe it with indigenous cultural forms.

Herein lies the difficult task of cultural theologians. It is to determine the significance of God and salvation in the original context of the New

Testament and then to 'translate' this message into the language and symbolism of the receiving culture. At the same time, the Gospel has often been a powerful force in transforming cultures themselves. This has been especially the case when it has come into contact with small-scale societies, but it has also been true to some extent in parts of Asia (as in India and Japan) where numerically Christians are only a small minority.

Theological cultural transformation is most evident in the adaptation of indigenous forms of liturgy and worship. The use of traditional chants and musical instruments for hymns, of traditional postures for prayer, of indigenous dress for the clergy, and so on, is in many countries well advanced. Traditional praise names for God have also been incorporated into liturgies. African peoples, in particular, have a rich variety of such names for God, which reflect their own cultural needs and situation. Indian theologians, on the other hand, have introduced into Christian theological vocabulary terms which are widely used in Indian religions – *sat**, *cit**, *ananda** (being, knowledge, bliss) as applied to the Trinity, or *avatar** to describe the incarnation.

Such terms may stand in need of some redefinition when used in theology, for the Christian meaning is seldom exactly the same as the original one. But they can be ways into theologizing by using the raw materials and terminology which are already to hand in the culture concerned, and which have a long and venerable history. Such terms are more than mere labels; they are also symbols in the sense defined earlier, in that they draw upon a depth of meaning which is part of the experience of the hearer. We shall discuss below two examples of such symbols, one from Africa, the other from India, which have been used by Christian theologians to explore the significance of Jesus in their own context.

AN AFRICAN EXAMPLE OF CULTURAL THEOLOGY

Probably the central feature of all African religion is the role of the ancestors. Ancestor veneration is a very important part of the total complex of African culture and may be regarded as the cement which holds African societies together. The ancestors have the right and authority to interfere in the affairs of the living, for ill if they are displeased and for good if they are well-disposed. They are also the guardians of morality and ritual. As Harry Sawyerr once put it, 'they are an all-pervading influence' and as such are the main factor in shaping the lives and destinies of their living descendants.

The ancestors do not fit very easily into Christian systematic theology, but they are so central to Africans that several African theologians have striven to interpret them in Christian terms. Harry Sawyerr and Edward Fashole-Luke, both from Sierra Leone, have found a role for them in the doctrine of the Communion of Saints – a dogma indeed acknowledged in the Creed but more often than not almost completely neglected in Western Protestant theology. Sawyerr argued that just as the African community embraces the living, the unborn and the dead, so the Church exists both on earth (the Church militant) and in heaven (the Church triumphant). So Christian teaching should emphasize the solidarity between the living and the dead. There is, he believed, theological and biblical warrant for prayers on behalf of the dead, and for the hope that the non-Christian ancestors could be incorporated into the Christian community. Fashole-Luke has argued in a similar way. For him the sacrifice of Jesus is all-embracing and reaches even to the non-Christian dead. The infinite worth of the death of Christ is, he believes, mediated to the dead through the sacraments of baptism and eucharist.

Other African theologians, like the Catholics Nyamiti and Bujo, have used the ancestor concept to elucidate christology in the context of African culture. For Nyamiti Christ may be regarded as Ancestor because, just as the human ancestor establishes a link between the spirit world and that of the living, so Jesus by His crucifixion and resurrection establishes a mystical link between God and the Christian community. Nyamiti believes that in Africa the relationship between God and Jesus is more understandable if regarded as one between Ancestor and Descendant than in the traditional Christian imagery of Father and Son.

Bujo agrees that the ancestors are central and inescapable to the African experience. For him Jesus is best understood as the 'Proto'* (that is, first) Ancestor, by which he means that Jesus fulfils all the characteristics of the ideal ancestor, but at the same time transcends them. The arguments of these theologians are at times intricate and complex (though no more so than those of Origen and Bultmann!), but they represent a genuine attempt to see Christian doctrine through the eyes of African religious culture and to work in symbols which are meaningful in the traditional cultural context.

AN INDIAN EXAMPLE OF CULTURAL THEOLOGY

African religion lacks any clear idea of an incarnation. Hinduism, however, has a very definite incarnationism. In popular Hinduism the god Vishnu (the Preserver) incarnates himself whenever the cycle of time reaches its lowest point. In the *Bhagavadgita** IV. 7–8 the Lord Krishna (one of Vishnu's incarnations) says: 'Whenever there is a decline of righteousness and a rise of unrighteousness then I incarnate myself for the protection of the good and the destruction of the wicked, for the establishment of righteousness I come into being from age to age.' There are many of these avatars, or incarnations, the last of which is still to come.

The concept of avatar is one which, not surprisingly, has interested Indian theologians. A. J. Appasamy, a South Indian bishop, based his understanding of Christian theology on the tradition in Hinduism called *bhakti**. In the *bhakti* tradition salvation comes through the personal devotion to a particular incarnation of God. Appasamy recognizes that there are differences between the Hindu concept of avatar and the incarnation in Christianity. For Christians the incarnation of Jesus is once for all, and Jesus lived a real flesh and blood existence. In Hinduism the avatars of Vishnu are more 'docetic'* since they belong to the world of *maya** (illusion) rather than the world of ultimate reality. But if these differences are properly appreciated, Appasamy believed that the avatar concept is useful in presenting the Christian message to those of Hindu background and culture.

These attempts to formulate a christology in terms of Jesus as Ancestor or of avatar may seem a long way from the New Testament description of Jesus as Lord or Son of Man, and still further from the metaphysical definitions of the person of Christ which we find in the creeds. However, what the writers referred to in this chapter are trying to do is to express their experience of Christ within the symbols and language of their own cultural context, to which people who share that cultural context can relate. This is surely what doing cultural theology is all about.

STUDY SUGGESTIONS

WORDS AND MEANINGS
1 Briefly define:
   (a) culture;
   (b) tradition;
   (c) *Weltanschauung*;
   (d) *Bhakti*.
2 Explain what is meant by:
   (a) particularity;
   (b) schizophrenia.

REVIEW AND CONTENT
3 What are the main factors which contribute to:
   (a) our context;
   (b) our culture?

STUDY SUGGESTIONS

4 What is meant by the statement that 'all cultures are in a sense God-given'?
5 What is the 'difficult task of cultural theologians'?

CONTEXTUAL APPLICATION AND DISCUSSION

6 What do you see as the main characteristics of your own culture, which make it distinctive? How far have they changed or been modified in your own lifetime?
7 How far is it true that in colonialized areas, some aspects of traditional culture 'go underground'? If you can, give examples.
8 What has been the impact on the culture of your own people of:
   (a) Christianity;
   (b) other indigenous religions;
   (c) urbanization;
   (d) industrialization;
   (e) colonialization;
   (f) immigration?
9 What traditional ideas and practices have been or could be used in developing a cultural Christian theology for your people?
10 (a) How far do you think the Hindu concept of avatar can be useful in conveying the meaning of the incarnation of Jesus?
   (b) How far do you think the African concept of the ancestors can become part of a valid Christian theology? (If you can, read the relevant literature listed on p. 105 before answering this question.)

6

Theologians in Society

SOCIAL GROUPS

In the creation narrative in the Book of Genesis God, having created man, says: 'It is not good for the man to live alone.' A Bantu* proverb expresses the same idea in a slightly different way: 'A person is only truly human within society.' It is a universal fact that all of us live within a family and a community. If we are to consider human experience as part of the raw material of doing theology, therefore, we shall have to take some account of the 'social sciences', those disciplines which make a study of human societies. Broadly speaking these fall into three main areas: those which are concerned with the development and functioning of social groups (sociology), those which deal with government and social control (politics) and those which examine material resources, wealth and production (economics).

Each one of us is a member of certain social groups. We belong to some because of our birth, for example our sex, our family (both immediate and extended), our ethnic group, our nation. These are beyond our control and cannot usually be changed. In some societies there may be other constraints because of birth. In India, for example, caste* is an accident of birth, justified in classical Hinduism as the reward or punishment for deeds committed in past incarnations, and caste may seriously hamper or greatly advantage an individual.

We may also acquire a social or economic status because of our birth – whether we are born into an élite or peasant family, whether we are rich or poor, and so on. These latter are groups from which an individual may eventually break out, especially in modern societies which are more fluid than traditional ones.

Our religion or (if we are Christian) our denomination is also inherited – we are 'born into' a Muslim, Catholic, Baptist, non-religious family. Religious adherence, though, may also become a matter of choice, and in practice in most countries conversion from one religion to another is possible (though this is not the case in some Muslim states where conversion from Islam is illegal).

In some countries our social and economic status may be determined by our race, as was the case in America before the Civil Rights Movement, and in South Africa under apartheid. Again, in many parts of Europe, and of the Third World itself, minorities are often subjected to discrimination which may make movement to a better standard of living or to positions of authority difficult. Thus in all societies, to one degree or another, some groups will be dominant and others subservient, some wealthy and others poor, some privileged and others marginalized.

SOCIAL CONTROL: POLITICS

All societies, if they are to function properly and in an orderly way, require means of exercising social control. Even the smallest groups have some kind of authority, usually with power vested in the chief or the elders. The effective exercise of control depends on sanctions, that is, laws which may punish those who deviate from accepted social behaviour. Thus some kind of government is necessary. This may vary. It may be a dictatorship (absolute rule by one person), or a democracy (in theory rule by the people, usually through chosen representatives) or anything between.

WEALTH AND PRODUCTION: ECONOMICS

All societies, furthermore, even the most simple, share out functions of work for the economic good of the group as a whole. For example, in the so-called 'hunting and gathering' societies it was usually the men who hunted and the women who gathered food. Division of labour on the grounds of sex becomes less rigid the more sophisticated the society, where emphasis comes to be more on training, skills and functions. No one person can perform every task necessary for life, and so functions are divided ('division of labour'). This will almost inevitably lead to 'class' structures; the occupations that are most valued will attract the most status and remuneration.

Over against this, however, is the fact that much wealth and ownership or property is not acquired by labour but inherited through birth. Where wealth is concentrated in the hands of relatively few it may, as Karl Marx pointed out, lead to the exploitation of the underprivileged workers by the privileged owners of production ('the capitalists').

THEOLOGIANS AS MEMBERS OF SOCIETY

Christians share not only in the membership of a particular Church (a society, or better an 'association', of believers in Christ), but also in membership of other social groupings – family, workplace, union, country, as well as any cultural, sporting or other society to which they may choose to belong. Their theological thinking will inevitably be influenced by their participation in these groupings within the wider society and, if their theology is to be at all relevant, it will have to address the kinds of issues which are thrown up by such participation.

Of course the Christians may seek to avoid such involvement and withdraw from society (like the hermits), or they may again try to form or join an exclusive closed community, separated from the world, made up of only those who believe the same as they do. But aside from the fact that it is becoming increasingly difficult to do this (the world at large will not leave us in peace most of the time!), even this very decision to withdraw from society implies a certain choice – it implies that the world as a whole is not important enough for Christians to get involved in. This is not, I think, a position which most Christians today would find it easy to accept, since it implies that this world is no longer God's world which they should be concerned about.

The various human groups to which we belong constantly challenge us to make ethical and political choices. This was so in the earliest days of Christianity. The teaching of Jesus is deeply concerned with people who are marginalized, the outcasts of society, the poor, and at times He also (by implication, if not always explicitly) makes a judgement on the political as well as the religious systems of His day. Paul's writings also address (though not usually head on) the ethical problems of Graeco-Roman society – the responsibilities of family members, of slaves and masters, of ruler and ruled.

The early Christians soon found themselves having to make the political choice whether or not to offer sacrifice to the emperor, and whether they could reconcile the demands of the state, in this and in other matters, with their faith in the Lordship of Christ. These were inescapable decisions which were thrust upon them because they lived a life of faith within a particular social and political context. They were also decisions which involved theological judgements on issues of a socio-political nature.

From the time of the Christianization of the Roman Empire in the fourth century various attempts were made to create a 'Christian society', that is, one which was governed by Christian principles, and this concept persisted in Europe until relatively recently. However, all such attempts are probably doomed from the start. The Church is a society to which a person belongs by choice, whereas one is a member of a nation from birth. There will therefore inevitably be a degree of conflict between the Church, which is committed to the extension of the Kingdom of God, and the state, whose main concerns are within the purely material realm.

There are probably few theologians today who would argue that a 'Christian society' is in practice possible. Indeed many would claim that the New Testament does not give us a blueprint for such a society, for it assumes that there is always something inherently evil in human nature and that therefore all human societies will be flawed to a greater or lesser degree. But, conversely, this does not mean that human society is not able to be improved by Christian action and witness, and this is one function of mission.

Christians, then, have always to live within a society which is to some extent alien to the ideals which the Christian faith holds up to them. In this context theology has a twofold task. Firstly, it has to evaluate critically the structure and outworking of society, its inter-personal and inter-group relationships, its politics, government and economics. Having done this, it will then need to assess equally critically how near to – or how far from – Christian ideals and attitudes these structures and outworkings of society are.

Social, political and economic analysis is therefore an essential task preliminary to theological evaluation. Not many theologians are trained to do these specialist tasks, and most of us will have to rely to a large extent on the findings of social scientists. It is important then to remember that the work of those who study the human and social sciences is extremely relevant to doing theology. The roles of sociology, politics and economics are interrelated, for all three are aspects of society as a whole. A sharp division between them is therefore somewhat artificial. This should be kept in mind as we now briefly examine examples of Third World theologies which attempt to grapple with issues caused by conflict between groups and with political and economic problems.

AFRICAN AND INDIAN EXAMPLES OF THEOLOGY ADDRESSING RACIAL DISCRIMINATION

One of the factors which has caused much conflict during this century and the last has been race. Human history has indeed often been the story of the domination of one racial group by another, and in Europe in the last century the fiction of the Aryan* race provided one impetus for World War II.

Since then we have witnessed the struggles for the rights of ethnic groups in many different parts of the world, as well as the continued exploitation of minorities such as the Australian Aborigines, South American Indians, tribal peoples in many parts of Asia, and many others. On many of these issues the Church seems to have had very little to say. But there are contexts in which Christian theologians have faced racial discrimination squarely and have made a theological critique of racial injustice. One such example is Black theology* in America. A more striking one is Black South African theology.

Until the liberalization of laws in South Africa in the 1980s, blacks lived in that country under draconian* laws of apartheid* (separate development) which restricted their civil liberties, place of residence, employment and education. Black South Africans had no vote (though they constitute about 80% of the population) and had been subjected to indignities and systematic exploitation. Against such a background Black theology arose during the early 1970s. Its main emphasis, which it took partly from the cultural-political movement known as Black Consciousness, was upon the humanity and dignity of being black in a country dominated by white values and white supremacy. For Black Consciousness blackness was less a matter of skin colour than of mental attitude and conscientization*. South African Black theology had many eloquent spokesmen – Allan Boesak, Manas Buthelezi and Desmond Tutu, for example, and more recently younger theologians like Itumeleng Mosala, and Buti Thlagale.

In essence it sought to answer the question, 'What role does Christian theology have to play in liberating blacks in South Africa from the unjust racial society in which they live?' For blackness for them has been a 'given', a framework which determines the whole of life. It means more than skin colour – though of course it includes that. It has meant exclusion from the benefits of life, being forced to live on the margins of society, and being subjected to suffering and exploitation. Black theology tried to rectify this situation by exposing the contradictions within society between rich and poor, oppressors and oppressed, white and black.

But Black theology did not seek only to improve the material life of blacks in a purely economic sense, because that would be to accept the white values of South African society as all-important. Rather it has advocated a completely different social order, a different structure, in which blacks are able to enjoy a full humanity, a wholeness of life within a society completely liberated from racial exploitation and oppression. This it tried to do from the theological base of the Christian view of creation, justice and redemption. Black theology played a significant role in the overthrow of apartheid and the establishment of democratic government in South Africa.

Social discrimination of a different kind has been addressed in a recent development in Indian Christian Theology. *Dalit** theology aims at exposing the evil of caste in Indian society, which has continued to play a significant role even within the Churches. The Aryan invasions of India during the second millennium BC resulted in the subjugation of the aboriginal peoples of India or their flight to the remoter areas. As Hinduism became consolidated during the period of the *Upanishads** (about 600–400 BC) a rigid social structure of caste took effect (it is perhaps significant that one of the words for caste, 'varna'*, means literally 'colour'). This effectively excluded the lowest caste, the *Sudras**, from religion through the doctrine that 'the gods speak only to the highest castes'. This dogma was reinforced by the creation myth in the Hindu scriptures (*Rig-Veda** X, 90) according to which the higher castes came into being from the mouth, arms and thighs of the primeval man, Purusha, but the *Sudras* came from his feet. Religious sanction was thus given to a social system which oppressed the lower strata of society.

If the lot of the *Sudras* was bad, far worse was that of those who were excluded from the caste system altogether, the *avarna** or outcastes (called harijans*, 'children of God', by Gandhi, and 'scheduled castes' in the Indian constitution). Some of their leaders prefer to use the term *dalit** to describe themselves, from a Sanskrit word meaning 'broken, oppressed' which is incidentally almost identical with the Hebrew word *dal**, which has a similar meaning. Today *dalits* make up about 20% of the Indian population, and between 60% and 70% of them are Christians. *Dalits* are left to do dirty and degrading work or are landless labourers. They have a very high illiteracy rate and 3.2 million of them live below the poverty line. *Dalits* – especially the women – are subjected to physical abuse, denied basic human rights, and have been systematically brain-washed into accepting their inferior status. Even the Christian Churches have connived at their oppression in the past.

Dalit theology seeks to speak on behalf of these oppressed peoples. It is a grass-roots theology of the people which tries to effect the liberation of *dalits* by ridding them of a servant mentality and emphasizing God's liberating presence in a world which has denied their true humanity and exploited them economically, socially and culturally. It is a new way of doing theology, and quite different from the more philosophical approach of earlier indigenous theologies in India, which tried to build bridges between Hindu thought and Christianity.

AN EXAMPLE OF FEMINIST THEOLOGY

Both Black theology and *Dalit* theology also draw attention to another group within the Churches who are often denied their full rights, namely women. Though Christianity has throughout history often been a powerful factor in advancing the status of women, their position in many societies is still depressed, and they are not infrequently regarded and treated as second-class citizens, within the Churches as well as outside. Women's value is often considered only in their relationship to men – usually as wives and mothers – rather than as persons and individuals in their own right. In many Churches the ministry of women is restricted.

Feminist theologies are a necessary counterbalance to this attitude.

Marianne Katoppo (though she avoids the term 'feminist') in her short book *Compassionate and Free* seeks to address the question, 'How do Asian women encounter God?' Katoppo is from Sulawesi (Celebes) in Indonesia, a country where Christians number only about 3% of the population. In male-dominated societies, both modern and traditional, women are seen (as she puts it) as 'other', and women's experiences of discrimination, subordination and domination are not taken account of. In the same way, a woman's personal experience of God is regarded as somehow less valid than that of men. Women are the property of men and valued only in relationship to their menfolk.

Cultural and religious factors often condition women towards accepting their subservient position, and all but a small number live under harsh conditions. In Asia 85% of women live in villages, and a significant percentage of girls are undernourished because the available food goes first to the men of the household. Women are also exploited physically and sexually both in the home and in the place of work. These facts should challenge us to rethink our theology in order to cast off its male-dominated and middle-class attitudes, and should cause us to consider more deeply the problems faced by women in society at large and in the Church in particular.

Marianne Katoppo argues that women have a right to be liberated from being seen as 'the threatening other' to men and instead should be appreciated for all their fullness and different gifts. She sees Mary as an example of creative submission to the will of God (not to the will of men), and points to the way in which the Bible often uses 'feminine' images to describe God. So she asks us to take women seriously in their own right as equal partners in the wholeness of God's creation and redemption. A valid theology for today cannot avoid tackling openly this issue of sexual discrimination.

AFRICAN AND KOREAN EXAMPLES OF THEOLOGY ADDRESSING POLITICAL ISSUES

Protests against racial, socio-religious and sexual discrimination are one way in which Christians attempt to come to grips with an evil in the world which, to one degree or another, affects all societies. This naturally leads us to the question of conflicts within nations themselves, and of the obligation of Christian thinkers to comment, favourably or unfavourably, on political systems and the way in which their countries are governed. This is not always easy, nor is it always so obvious which side of the political fence Christians should be on.

While there can be no real argument that discrimination against one particular group, on any grounds whatever, is morally and theologically wrong, the issue at the level of state institutions is seldom so simple, and

Christians have often been divided over such issues. Is it, for example, justifiable on theological grounds to support a 'one-party state' in which all political control is vested in the ruling party and no official opposition is permitted? Many have claimed, rightly, that such a system curtails liberty of conscience and is therefore unjustifiable. Others have responded that democracy as practised in Europe and America is unsuitable for poorer countries, and that the needs of national development demand the unity of a strong government which can take decisions in the interest of the nation as a whole.

Again, is a 'capitalist' or a 'socialist' system nearer to the Christian ideal? It has been argued that capitalism leads to such unequal distribution of wealth and exploitation of workers that it cannot be accepted by Christians. Others have responded to this that capitalism in fact creates more wealth which can then be shared, so that in the final analysis even the poor become better off.

There are no easy solutions to these rather theoretical debates, nor is there any final and absolute Christian answer to the issue of differing political systems. But what all Christians, and especially those who seek to do theology, are obliged to do is to examine and analyse the results of the political systems in their own societies. They are duty bound to support whatever in the political set-up supports the struggle for greater humanity and a better quality of life. At the same time (even though in some states this may be personally very costly) they must expose dehumanizing and degrading aspects of government and those which curtail basic rights and liberties. And they must be prepared to do this on behalf of all who suffer, whether the victims are Christian or not.

Some states have attempted to institute political ideologies which try to approximate to Christian principles. Former President Julius Nyerere of Tanzania, himself a devout Catholic, propounded the doctrine of *Ujamaa**, which sought to develop rural communities into villages large enough to justify the provision of such services as clean water supplies, education, health, and so on, and thus radically to improve the quality of life. *Ujamaa* also sought to counter uncontrolled urbanization and to encourage self-reliance and community co-operation.

Many theologians, some of them with experience of living in *Ujamaa* communities, enthusiastically supported *Ujamaa* and urged the Church to become actively involved in it. While we cannot detract from the very positive values of the ideal of *Ujamaa*, it is clear that in practice there were also costs in human terms, for example, in the forcible removal of people from their traditional areas and in the opportunities which the system gave to political corruption. These aspects of *Ujamaa* did not receive the same attention from Christian thinkers. An authentic

Christian theology has to examine both sides of the issue if it is to be credible and keep its integrity.

An example of a different kind comes from Korea. Korea is a country which has suffered from political domination from outside for much of its modern history, and this culminated in a bitter civil war in the 1950s which resulted in the formation of North (Communist) Korea and South (capitalist) Korea. After a period of domination by Western missionary teaching, Korean Christians began to formulate a theology of their own. In the 1970s some of the Churches in the South, which had until then taken a strong anti-communist stance, began to rethink their position during the particularly repressive regime of President Park.

Thus *Minjung** theology arose. *Minjung* means 'the people', and *Minjung* theology was a theology which affected and sought to speak on behalf of the rural and urban workers, peasants and students – in fact, all who were politically oppressed. *Minjung* took the sufferings of the people very seriously and focused upon their struggle for a truly human existence. It favours a socialist emphasis and works for radical social change to alleviate the oppression of those who are exploited. It also believes that democracy cannot be attained except by the reunification of North and South Korea into one nation. It sees the national division as reflecting the bigger problem of conflict between world powers and ideologies. The key to the coming of the Kingdom of God is therefore reconciliation, in which the Church has a vital role to play. *Minjung* theology shows how Christian theologians can examine critically the political structures in which they live, subjecting them to the light of the Gospel and exposing what is perceived as evil in them.

A LATIN AMERICAN EXAMPLE OF THEOLOGY ADDRESSING ECONOMIC ISSUES

Let us now turn to examples of theologies which focus primarily on the economic factor. The most well known is the theology of liberation, which arose in South America during the 1960s. (Some writers use the term 'theology of liberation' in a very wide and vague way, but for purposes of clarity I shall here restrict its use to Latin America where it originated.)

Liberation theology was a new approach to theology, which sought to emphasize the poor. While it did not ignore the sense of liberation as personal salvation, it was much more concerned to stress liberation as 'self-realization' and as freedom from degrading social, political and economic conditions. The key factor here was to awaken the conscience of the oppressed ('conscientization') to realize their condition for what it was and to assert positively their own self-dignity (in much the same way as Black theology and *Dalit* theology do in different contexts). The oppressed then become actively involved in the process of their own liberation from socio-economic powerlessness.

A primary task for liberation theology is to determine the causes of the oppression of the poor. Its starting point is therefore the human situation rather than Christian tradition. This situation needs to be examined and analysed, and to do this liberation theology makes use of the tools of the social sciences, and especially of the economic theory of Karl Marx. According to Marx, economics – the methods of production – determines the characteristics of society as a whole, its politics, art, religion, morality, and so on.

In a capitalist society the owners of the means of production are the élite few – wealthy industrialists, landowners – who exploit the labour of the workers for their own benefit. This inevitably leads to class conflict between the workers and the owners as the former seek to free themselves from exploitation. Human history is thus a series of conflicts and of resolutions of conflict (called 'dialectic'). Since exploitation of the workers is part and parcel of the capitalist system, this system cannot be reformed but has to be overthrown by revolution. Marx believed that history was moving, by a succession of such revolutions, towards a classless society.

Liberation theology has used this Marxist social analysis to address unequal structures which create poverty in Latin America. Poverty, on this view, is not natural: it is always caused by greed and injustice and by the ruthless exploitation of the workers. This injustice, furthermore, is reinforced by 'institutional violence', that is, the use of the police, law courts and security forces to keep the poor under the control of the élites. In theological terms this constitutes a sinful situation, an evil structure, which committed theologians should vigorously oppose.

What liberation theologians are trying to do, therefore, is not simply to make their societies a little more just and equal, but rather to change them completely. This can only be done by revolutionary action (praxis) and by the Church deliberately taking on an 'option for the poor' to redeem society from unequal political and social structures. Liberation theology can therefore describe itself as 'orthopraxis' or right action rather than orthodoxy (right belief). Its aim is the transformation of society and the humanization of people suffering injustice and oppression due to economic and political exploitation.

Liberation theology's findings are indeed applicable to many Third World countries which have similar conditions to those in South America. In Asia, for example, only between 10% and 15% have an adequate standard of living. Of the remaining 85% to 90% who are poor, many exist well below subsistence level in homelessness and hunger. In Africa the average income was calculated in the 1990s at about US$200 per person per annum, and this is very unevenly distributed. Poverty, exploitation for economic ends, and gross inequalities are world-wide problems which demand the attention of theologians.

THEOLOGY AND WORLD ECONOMICS

But economic exploitation is not only an internal matter within nation states. It occurs on the largest scale in the exploitation of the material and natural resources of one country by another, and especially by the so-called 'multi-national corporations'. These are large industrial and business concerns which invariably have their headquarters in the West, but which exploit the cheap labour and raw materials of the underdeveloped world. Because many Third World countries are forced to rely very heavily on such multi-nationals to manufacture and market their resources, these corporations are able to exercise political as well as economic control over the poorer nations.

Another important factor has been that of debts owed to the West. These are sometimes so great that much of a nation's wealth is taken up in paying off the interest alone. In the 1980s Latin American countries owed the United States $400 billion, and the situation of African states was little better. Aid from international organizations is often given only on the condition that harsh economic measures are taken. For example, the International Monetary Fund or World Bank have demanded devaluation of the local currency, which affects the poorest people worst of all and makes their lives yet more intolerable.

Clearly these are matters of immense moral, and therefore theological, importance. Theologians cannot ignore addressing such problems of economic 'neo-colonialism', and the wider issue of how developing countries can achieve economic self-sufficiency and a just distribution of wealth, so that a truly human existence is possible for all.

The social, political and economic context forms a 'given' for theologians, which they cannot ignore without risk of becoming irrelevant to their people. Whether they begin from the usually accepted sources of Christian tradition and then seek to apply these to their own context (the traditional way of doing theology) or whether they reverse this process and begin by analysing the context before seeking to relate it to those sources of tradition (the method, among others, of liberation theology) is a question about which there is no unanimity. However, to devalue or, worse, to ignore the social, political and economic structures in which we work is seriously to limit the practical usefulness of our theological thinking.

STUDY SUGGESTIONS

WORDS AND MEANINGS

1. Briefly define each of the following as used in this chapter:
   (a) sociology;
   (b) social control;
   (c) class;
   (d) race;
   (e) Aryan;
   (f) *Dalits*;
   (g) *Ujamaa*.
2. Explain what is meant by:
   (a) basic human rights;
   (b) social analysis;
   (c) capitalism;
   (d) orthopraxis.
3. What is meant by 'a different social order, a different structure' in the context of Black theology in South Africa?

REVIEW OF CONTENT

4. What are the main factors which lead to division between different groups of people in any society?
5. What is meant by 'ethical and political choices'? What are the main such choices facing the Churches in your country?
6. Why is it necessary to take social, political and economic analysis into account in doing theology?
7. What are the main ideas presented by each of the following theologies, and in which countries have they arisen?
   (a) Black theology;
   (b) *Dalit* theology;
   (c) *Minjung* theology;
   (d) liberation theology.
   How valid do you think these ideas are for theology in your own country, and why?

CONTEXTUAL APPLICATION AND DISCUSSION

8. Consider the advantages and disadvantages of different forms of capitalism and socialism. What system is current in your own country today? Which form, if any, do you think might be more suitable, and why?
9. Is it ever possible for wealthy and privileged Christians to understand and identify with poor and underprivileged people? If so, how?

10 Is a fully Christian society ever possible? If not, what sort of society should Christians be seeking to create?
11 What is the place and status of women as compared with that of men in your country, in regard to:
    (a) education;
    (b) level of employment;
    (c) positions of authority in government and commerce;
    (d) positions in the Churches?
    What steps, if any, do you think Christians should take to improve the position and status of women? If you can, read the book by Marianne Katoppo listed on p. 105, and note why she feels that women are treated as inferior to men in many countries. How far are her arguments valid for your own country?
12 How true is it to say that poverty and injustice are not 'natural', but are always the result of misuse of power and social structures? Consider your answer in relation to the situation in your own country.
13 What theological questions are raised by the influence of multi-national commercial corporations, and by the debt incurred by developing countries which have received 'aid' from the West?

7

The Problem of History

LINEAR AND CYCLICAL VIEWS OF HISTORY

Christianity has rightly been called a 'historical religion'. Along with Islam, it originated in the ancient Middle East and had its source in ancient Judaism. The Jewish Scriptures, our Old Testament, developed a very distinctive view of history. History, according to the prophets, was a process of the growth and development of the people of God, whose story was under the immediate control and guidance of God Himself. From time to time, at critical periods in their history, God revealed Himself in special acts of salvation and judgement.

The New Testament writers accepted and developed this view of history as the acts of God. The Christian faith depended upon certain events, accepted as actual happenings in time and space, through which God revealed His purposes. Thus the birth, ministry, death and resurrection of Jesus as described in the Gospels provided the foundation material for the theologizing of the Epistles. St Luke elaborated in the Book of Acts the idea (which was no doubt the common understanding of the early Christians) that the spread of the Gospel was the continuation of the story of the people of God and of the actions of God in human history. All the New Testament writers are fundamentally agreed that the world is progressing to an *eschaton**, an end point which will mean the finality of human history as we know it and the consummation of the Kingdom of God.

This view of history contrasts sharply with what we find in many traditions from other parts of the world. Eastern thought, for example, tends not to regard history as moving to an ultimate goal but rather as a perpetual series of ages or epochs. Some writers have illustrated this difference by comparing the Judaeo-Christian view of history to a straight line (called the linear understanding of history), and the Eastern view to a circle which has no beginning and no end (the cyclical understanding).

The difference can also be illustrated in their different concepts of incarnation. In Christianity there is only one incarnation, which suffices for all time, and it is theologically inconceivable for a Christian that the Son of God should become flesh for a second time. In Hinduism on the other hand, as we have seen, Vishnu becomes incarnate in each one of the cycles of time. It has been argued that the primal or traditional religions (such as African religions) share with

Hinduism the concept of time as cyclical. Time in these societies is marked by recurring festivals, agricultural rituals and rites of passage, and there is no concept of an *eschaton* in the Christian sense. It is, of course, true that the Western idea of development and progress (which itself may be a result of Christian thought), and the discoveries by nuclear and other physicists, have in recent years significantly modified the cyclical understanding of time.

In practice it is quite possible to hold both views of a linear and a cyclical view of time together, however inconsistent this may appear to be. But however that may be, the idea of history as linear time is an important factor in the Christian world-view, and allied to this is the equally important assumption that God acts to reveal Himself in events which take place in human history. Christianity also assumes that certain events, especially the incarnation, crucifixion and resurrection, are more important than others.

This view of history, which almost all theologians would accept in broad terms, however, raises a number of difficulties in respect of both 'sacred history'* (that is, history through which God is believed to reveal Himself) and 'secular history' (history which does not, apparently, fall into this category). The most important of these are perhaps:

1. How can we be sure of what happened in history, especially in sacred history?

2. If revelation takes place in biblical or Christian history, why should it not also take place in 'secular' history, that is, in the history of non-Christian peoples?

3. How, in any case, can we recognize and interpret correctly the meaning of revelation that is presented to us in historical events?

THE PROBLEM OF THE ACCURACY OF THE BIBLE

Our first question presents the theologians with their most pressing challenge in respect of the Bible itself. The rise of biblical criticism led scholars to read and examine the Bible in the same way as other ancient writings. Firstly, there was the special problem of miracles, some of which appeared to be so out of the ordinary as to be of very doubtful historicity*. Serious questions also began to emerge when the Bible was compared to other ancient literature. Some of these historical problems do indeed begin to disappear when we use the right hermeneutical tools and recognize the various kinds of literary categories which are being employed. Genesis 1, for example, will be seen as myth, not scientific history, Jonah may be understood as a parable rather than a narrative, Daniel as apocalyptic, and so on.

But other historical problems in the Bible are more persistent. For many central revelational events (the Exodus, for example, or the resurrection of Jesus) we have no evidence at all outside the Bible. Even the evidence for the life and ministry of Jesus apart from the Gospels, convincing enough though it may be to establish beyond reasonable doubt the essential fact of His existence, is very small indeed. Thus the Bible remains very largely our only real evidence. And, as has been quite rightly argued, the writers of the Bible had their own beliefs and convictions which they wanted to advance, and they cannot therefore be regarded as in any sense impartial witnesses. How can theologians respond to these problems?

Some Christians respond by simply stating their belief that since the Bible is the Word of God it must be true and free in all respects from error, including historical error. This view has the advantage of giving a straightforward dogmatic answer to the problem. However, it will scarcely satisfy people who are genuinely concerned about the very real historical problems which are evident in the Bible.

At the opposite end of the spectrum there have been people who have argued that history does not really matter, and that faith does not have to rely on historical facts. Bultmann, for example, argued that the 'facts' about Jesus cannot be known from the New Testament documents, for our Gospels are not history in the modern sense. They are essentially preaching, *kerygma* (the Greek word for the preached message). All that the New Testament documents tell us is what the early Christians believed about Jesus, not what He actually was and did. So for Bultmann faith cannot depend upon history, and the Christian commitment is not dependent on the findings of historians.

There is clearly an element of truth in all this. The Gospels are indeed statements of faith in a sense, and they certainly do reflect what the early disciples understood Jesus to be. But Bultmann's view also has its difficulties. In particular, it tends to reduce the Christian message to a kind of timeless 'myth', the historical basis for which is unimportant, and the historical figure of Jesus thus loses much of its significance. Furthermore it is obvious that the first Christians were very interested indeed in 'what happened', otherwise they would hardly have bothered to remember and write down in the Gospels what Jesus is thought to have done and said! And since we all live in human history, it is not unreasonable to expect that God would reveal Himself through concrete historical events which men and women can experience.

So the kerygmatic view of biblical history is basically just as unsatisfactory as the literalist one. There is no way, if we are to do theology, that we can avoid facing squarely the problem of the relationship between faith and history. How do we 'get at' the history of Jesus, and indeed at the history of the people of God as contained in the Bible?

The first thing that we can say is that there is a reasonable degree of certainty about the essential historicity of the main events on which our faith is based. Few scholars would deny, for instance, that the Exodus narrative is based on some historical event of deliverance. Though they may argue about the date and route, whether or not all the tribes were involved, and other details, the fact of such a deliverance is too deeply ingrained in the religious traditions of Israel to be seriously denied historical validity.

The same is true of the life of Jesus. Though New Testament scholars may debate whether Jesus did or did not say and do particular things, or say or do them in exactly the way they are recorded in the Gospels, there is little doubt that the Christian message was based on certain known facts. These facts occur again and again in the apostolic preaching preserved in the Book of Acts, and also in the snatches of creeds contained in some of the Epistles (see e.g. 1 Cor. 15.3–11; Rom. 10.9). Thus while the details of the story of the people of God may be argued over (and the position we take here will be largely determined by our view of the Bible), the broad parameters can confidently be accepted as historical.

In one sense 'faith' always demands an element of risk. If all that we believe as Christians could be scientifically proved to the satisfaction of everyone, then faith would no longer be faith in the Christian sense. For as the writer to the Hebrews puts it, 'Faith is the assurance of things hoped for, the conviction of things not seen' (Heb. 11.1).

Not all the 'events' of Christian belief are of the same kind. Some, like the crucifixion, have sufficient 'objective' evidence to support them that it would be quite unreasonable to doubt their factual historicity. Others, such as the virgin birth or the resurrection – or indeed what we call 'miracles' in general – are of quite a different order. These are not subject to the same kind of historical verification and are in a sense events which transcend what normally happens. They are therefore more articles of faith than provable events of history. This does not mean that they did not happen, but rather that they belong to a different sphere of experience and knowledge than can be reasonably verified by historical investigation.

With regard to these events theologians will differ about what to make of them. One theologian may understand, for instance (see chapter 1), the ascension of Jesus in a literal sense, while another may see in it not so much an historical happening in the normal sense of the word as a powerful symbolic means of conveying the spiritual truth of Christ's Lordship over the world. We are here beginning to address our third question, of how we correctly interpret revelation which is presented to us in historical form.

We have suggested that even in the Bible some events reveal more of

God to us than others. Let us put this in a more concrete way: are the lists of unclean animals in the Book of Leviticus, or those of the returned exiles in Ezra-Nehemiah, revelation in the same sense as the story of the Exodus or the crucifixion? There is no doubt that they served a cultural and historical purpose which was very important to the Jews (and indeed still is to Orthodox Judaism). But probably most of us would agree that Christian theology would not be significantly worse off if they had not been included in Scripture.

Again, to some extent it is true that what is important to individual Christians (or to the Church as a whole at any given time) may depend upon the particular spirituality or needs of that given moment (or what the needs of the Church are during that particular period of time). There are, however, also central events which are of paramount importance to the Church as a whole at all times.

CHRISTIAN HISTORY

Up to this point we have been discussing a particular kind of history, that is, the history of salvation as presented to us in the Bible. But (as we have argued in chapter 4) most Christians would agree that God's acts in history did not stop around AD 120. Consequently the whole story of the Church must in some way be a record of God's continuing activity in the world, and therefore constitute a valid source for doing theology.

This is not to claim that everything in Christian history is good or an outworking of God's purposes, any more than the periods of apostasy* in ancient Israel or lapses in the early Church (e.g. Acts 5.1–11) were. Certainly the misuse of Christianity in the interests of colonialization in many parts of the world and in massacres of Jews can hardly be regarded as part of divine revelation. Christian history provides raw materials only, which need to be critically evaluated and judged before they can be of use to theologians.

WORLD HISTORY AS REVELATION

Can we not go further than this? Can it not also be argued that God is at work in all human history? Theologians have traditionally divided history into 'sacred' and 'secular' history, with only the former being usually taken as a legitimate source for Christian theology. But this view is not very easy to defend. Even the Old Testament recognizes God's activity within Gentile nations, and passages like Genesis 1–11 show the universal application of God's providence. Unless we make the unacceptable assumption that God is not interested in anyone apart from Christians, we can scarcely avoid the conclusion that in some way God is at work in, and in control of, the history of all peoples and nations.

If this is so, then does it not also lead us to the conclusion that all peoples' histories are in a sense revelation? This point was forcefully argued by a group of African scholars at an important conference in Nigeria in 1969. 'We believe', they said, 'that God, the Father of our Lord Jesus Christ, Creator of heaven and earth, Lord of history, has been dealing with mankind at all times and in all parts of the world.' Mercy Amba Oduyoye, a Ghanaian theologian, would see the activity of God in African history, especially in political deliverance from colonialism. 'It is clear', she writes, drawing on the Exodus theme, 'from their political deliverance that the redemption of the community from unjust systems is not outside God's providence, that what God found necessary to do for Israel God has found necessary to do for the colonial peoples of Africa, and is doing for those held in bondage inside Africa.'

The same view has been advanced by the Taiwanese theologian C. S. Song. He argues that we study the history of Israel because we believe that 'God is in it'. In the same way God is 'in' all human history upon earth and therefore, as Song puts it, 'the data and events we encounter there constitute the subject matter of theological enquiry'. If we do not seek to ask the question of what God is doing in all human history, we shall be guilty of running away from the concrete acts of God in the world. The Indian theologian M. M. Thomas believed that there is general agreement that 'God is present in the Asian evolution and His judging redemptive work is essentially dynamic'.

But if God has been at work in the history of all peoples then He must also be at work in human history here and now, for He is the God of the present as well as of the past. The black South African theologian Allan Boesak, writing from within a situation of racial and political oppression, believed that God is at work in the social and political revolutions of our time, and that any attempt to create a better world is part of God's purposes and demands our active participation. Theology is thus essentially orthopraxis, action on the part of God against all forms of oppression. God is therefore at work and reveals Himself in the activity of all people (not just Christians) in working for liberation and true humanity.

The clearest statement of this position has come from the Latin American theology of liberation. According to this view theology always exists in a specific time, place and special context, and in that sense all theology may be described as 'historical'. (In much liberation theology 'historical' means not 'existing in the past' but 'existing in the present as part of the flow of history in which we share, the reality of the contextual situation now'.) Theology is present action which is meant to change the present oppressive situation.

From this standpoint all history is salvation history, for the people of God is all of humanity, not just the Church. Indeed some have argued that the special 'people of God' is not the Church but the poor. As a leading Latin American theologian has put it, 'God is a liberating God revealed only in the concrete historical context of the poor and oppressed.'

These problems do not have an easy solution. It would probably be difficult for most Christians to give up the conviction that there is something 'special' in the pivotal events of the Bible and (probably) in Christian history. At the same time, the Bible itself supports the rightness of those who claim that God is revealed in all human history and that He has special care for the poor and oppressed. Part of the theologian's task is to reconcile these two statements in delicate balance.

INTERPRETING HISTORY

This brings us to our third question: How can we first recognize, and then interpret correctly, the acts of God presented to us in history? Some historians (like Trevelyan) believed that history is intrinsically meaningless, while others (like Toynbee) have attempted to construct elaborate systems which they see as a pattern for world history. Both leave no place for God in history. This option is not open to Christian theologians. However difficult the task, they have to try to make sense of history from the standpoint of what they know and experience about God.

Making sense of biblical history is the easier task, for more often than not there is an interpretation of biblical events given us within Scripture itself. The Old Testament Torah and the Prophets, for example, interpret and reinterpret events like the Exodus time and again – it is one of the great 'sermon texts' of the Old Testament. The New Testament can also fairly accurately be described as an interpretation of the life, death and resurrection of Jesus. There is a sense in which the Bible is often its own interpreter. We are not, of course, always obliged to agree with what Amos or Isaiah say about the Exodus, or even with what Paul or John say about the cross. But neither are we left completely to our own devices in trying to fathom the meaning of these events.

With post-biblical history the case is different. There will probably be no complete agreement as to the theological meaning of events like the persecution of the early Church or the destruction of North African Christianity by the Muslims. Nor, on the other side, is it easy to find any theological meaning in the persecution of Jews by Christians or the often unholy alliance between the Christian missions and the colonial powers. It is still more difficult to find meaning in the horrifying events of world history in the twentieth century – Auschwitz, Hiroshima or Sharpeville.

But Christian theologians must take their stand on the conviction that God is Lord of all human history and that He may be found in the story of all peoples. It is part of their task therefore to struggle to make sense of the events of history through their own eyes, from their own context, and in the light of their own experience of faith.

STUDY SUGGESTIONS

WORDS AND MEANINGS

1. Briefly define:
   (a) eschaton;
   (b) kerygma;
   (c) miracle;
   (d) apostasy.
2. Explain what is meant by the 'essential historicity' of the events described in the New Testament.
3. What are the differences in each case, between:
   (a) the cyclical and the linear ideas of time;
   (b) sacred history and secular history;
   (c) narrative and parable.

REVIEW OF CONTENT

4. (a) What is the distinctive understanding of history that is developed in the Bible?
   (b) In what ways does this differ from other understandings of time and history?
5. What arguments have been used to support the view that God acts in the history of all peoples at all times?

CONTEXTUAL APPLICATION AND DISCUSSION

6. Is the idea that certain events actually happened essential to the Christian faith? If so, why?
7. How would you reply to someone who claimed that because the virgin birth of Jesus and His resurrection are unprovable, they are therefore unbelievable?
8. How far can the distinction between sacred history and secular history be sustained? In what ways, if any, are they likely to overlap?

STUDY SUGGESTIONS

9 By what criteria can we distinguish whether or not God reveals Himself:
   (a) in the history of all peoples;
   (b) in revolutionary movements;
   (c) in the liberation of the poor and oppressed?
10 If God reveals Himself through history, how can we make theological sense of human tragedies and natural disasters?
11 If God works through the history of the Church, how can we explain the role that Christian missions have often played in colonialism?

8

Philosophies and Religions

The *Concise Oxford Dictionary* defines philosophy as 'love of knowledge, especially that which deals with ultimate reality'. In this section we shall consider systems of thought which seek to describe the nature of reality in so far as they affect the task of theology. In so doing we shall bear in mind that each of us looks at the world from a particular standpoint, and in that respect has a 'philosophy', whether this is explicit or not.

THE IMPACT OF GREEK THOUGHT ON EARLY CHRISTIANITY

The earliest preachers of Christianity were Jews, and because of that the foundations of our faith were seen through the religious outlook of the Palestinian Judaism of the first century. But Judaism outside of Palestine (and even to some extent within it) had already, before the birth of Christianity, come into contact with the hellenistic world, the world of Greek thought and culture. Already, as we have seen, much of the Old Testament had been translated into Greek, and Jewish thinkers, like the famous Philo of Alexandria, had begun to rethink Judaism in terms of hellenism.

Palestinian Christianity soon became somewhat unimportant as the Church became predominantly Gentile. The centres of Christianity, especially after the fall of Jerusalem in AD 70, shifted away from Palestine to new centres in Asia Minor, North Africa and southern Europe. It was here that the earliest coherent theologies began to take shape, theologies which we call 'patristic', i.e. of the church 'Fathers'.

The expansion of Christianity coincided with a resurgence of ancient religious cults (Mithraism, for example) and of Greek philosophy, represented especially by the Stoics*, the Epicureans* and, above all, influenced by the thought of Plato*. Greek philosophy originally had its roots in Greek religion. While it had gradually separated from religion, it retained its emphasis upon the 'Absolute', the essential unity of the universe, and the concept of a principle (Reason or *Logos*) behind all reality.

In the formative period Greek philosophy influenced the task of doing Christian theology in many ways. All the Greek church Fathers accepted the primary importance of reason, and the insistence upon exact and precise definitions which characterized Greek ways of thinking. There was consequently a tendency to play down the role of experience, and to assume that because someone has defined reality they have therefore comprehended and fully grasped it. The influence of Plato's concept of ideas* (or forms), which taught that behind the world of appearances which we perceive there are 'ideal' realities which remain unchanged, became extremely important. Concepts like this could readily be incorporated into Christianity through the doctrine that Christ the *Logos* (a term already used by John at the beginning of his Gospel) was the 'seed' which enlightened the wise men of Greek tradition. As one church Father put it, 'What is Plato but Moses speaking in the language of Athens?'

The revival of Plato's philosophy by Plotinus (AD 205–70) and others, called Neoplatonism, further influenced early Christian theology. Though he was not a Christian, Plotinus had studied with Origen, and it has been claimed that he had more influence on early Christian theology than anyone else apart from Augustine. Plotinus taught that the Absolute (God) was without all distinctions, and could be known by intellectual contemplation. He accepted Plato's theory that the world is only a shadow of the real world of ideas.

The first few centuries were also, as we have noted in chapter 3, the period of the great heresies. The orthodox theologians used the tools of Greek philosophy to attack the heretics. Perceptions which were based in the first instance on the conviction that Christ was Lord now came to be more and more explicitly and logically defined in the terminology of the Greek philosophers. In consequence we have the great credal statements seeking to define the nature of Christ in terms like *homoousios**, *hypostasis**, *prosopon**, and so on. All such words were imported into theology from philosophical discourse, many had first been used by the Gnostics, and very few were found in the New Testament.

In fact, of course, the church Fathers could scarcely do otherwise than employ the language and thought-forms of their time in trying to make explicit their understanding of the significance of Jesus. Like all of us, they had to use whatever terms and ideas were available to them and comprehensible to the people of their own time – the fact that most Christians today can make very little of this kind of terminology is really our problem and not theirs!

But the difficulty for theology becomes compounded when the expression of faith of an earlier age is assumed to be universally valid for all times. In practice the Church has generally recognized this problem. While it accepted in the main the creeds of the first six centuries as valid expressions of Christian belief, later theologians have not hesitated to use quite different philosophical frameworks than those of Platonic philosophy in their own expositions of Christian doctrine.

The medieval schoolmen, for example, especially Thomas Aquinas, were much more influenced by the other main figure in ancient Greek philosophy, Aristotle.

Much modern theology owes rather more to Idealism*, and especially to Kant. It is unnecessary here to go into detail of the way in which different philosophies have been used in Christian theology. It is sufficient to say that theology cannot really operate in a philosophical vacuum, and has usually adopted (though indeed often with significant modifications) a philosophical framework of one kind or another within which to interpret Christian thought. It would, however, probably also be true to say that the marriage between philosophy and theology is today much more fragile than it has ever been.

PHILOSOPHY AND THEOLOGY: TWO MODERN EXAMPLES

In the twentieth century two movements in philosophy in particular significantly influenced theology. The first of these is Existentialism* (though some professional philosophers would deny that existentialism is properly a philosophical system since, as we shall see, it is basically anti-rational). Existentialism may be traced back to the Danish writer Søren Kierkegaard (1813–55). It has influenced modern Judaism (especially in the work of Martin Buber) as well as Christianity, and has also found expression in literature – indeed one of the best ways to 'get inside' existentialism is to read the novels of authors such as Dostoievsky and Sartre.

Existentialists believe that objective, impersonal thinking cannot be applied to the human situation since we 'exist' before we become a 'scientific object' to be investigated. Individuals, the 'subjects', are by their very nature people who exist, and who are therefore subjectively involved, concerned for their own being. Truth is therefore subjective: it is what is true for me, what I as a person am passionately committed to. We discover ourselves only in personal commitment.

For Heidegger, one of the most influential of modern existentialists, we are 'aroused to authentic existence' by ultimate situations, that is, situations of crisis which demand a decision from us. He believed that the ultimate crisis facing human beings was the threat of death: the realization of our own mortality which causes us to direct our commitment towards the future. Existentialism is in one sense 'anti-rational'; but it is also passionately concerned with each individual person, with their self-commitment and their need to make critical decisions.

Though not specifically Christian, existentialism has played a significant role as a framework for many theologians in the twentieth century, most notably Bultmann and, in a modified way, Paul Tillich.

For Bultmann Jesus is the 'one who makes authentic, properly human, existence a possibility for man'. This call to decision comes through the preaching of the Christian message (the *kerygma*). Tillich believed that pure existentialism was impossible because all human speech, if it is to communicate at all, has to deal in 'universals', that is, things which have meaning not just for each individual but for everyone. Nevertheless he believed that existentialism correctly guided Christian theologians to begin their work by making an analysis of the human condition in order to discover what questions were of ultimate concern to people as individual human beings.

Existentialism has been largely a philosophical movement in continental Europe, though its method of beginning with the human situation is not irrelevant to the Third World. Theologians more concerned with political issues, for example liberation theologians, have criticized it because it has seemed to them to deal exclusively with the inner experience of individuals and to have neglected those issues which concern the community as a whole – poverty, unjust structures, discrimination, and so on.

To address such socio-political issues these theologians, and others in different parts of the world, have opted for a philosophical framework which draws upon the 'dialectical materialism'* of Karl Marx. We have looked briefly at Marxism on p. 65. There we noted that Marx was basically atheistic, regarding religions as a creation of rulers for use as a tool to suppress the workers. Though Marx's social analysis has been used to good effect by liberation theology, one of the main problems in adopting a thoroughgoing Marxist framework for Christian theology is how to overcome the obvious contradiction between an atheistic philosophy and a theistic religious belief system.

THE POSTMODERN* CONDITION

In the second half of the twentieth century a different approach began to emerge in the Western world, which both built on modernism and at the same time rejected it. Modernism, which mainly derived from rationalism and the Enlightenment, thus led into what came to be called 'the postmodern condition'. Postmodernism is not a clearly defined philosophy, and indeed some of the ideas which it embraces antedate postmodernism as such. It is basically a revolt against the claims of authority, and especially against the assumption that knowledge can be neutral and objective. It rejects any system which claims to have absolute and universally valid truth (what it calls a 'grand narrative' or 'metanarrative'). Postmodernists therefore deny that there can be any comprehensive explanatory framework or universally valid reasoning. Claims to truth are, postmodernists argue, simply ways by which the powerful manipulate the oppressed. It therefore seeks to 'deconstruct' such claims by the 'hermeneutic of suspicion', that is, to question received wisdom and commonly held assumptions, and to expose what it sees as false claims by pointing out the hidden agendas on which they are based. There are thus no objectively true positions, there are only options ('little or personal narratives'). There is therefore a plurality of viewpoints, each of which is equally valid within its own context, but not valid in all contexts. Language in which these little narratives are expressed, according to this view, is simply a construction of a particular society and cannot be valid for all. The consequence of this position (which also lies behind the 'reader-response' approach to the Bible) is that a text does not have a fixed meaning. Logically it also rules out meaningful communication across these various contextual languages.

Postmodernism has spawned a variety of theological positions, mainly in the Western world, which has been affected in the last few decades by the shaking of old certainties. Some of these theological trends (but by no means all) have been helpful. One positive consequence has been the questioning of the claim to neutrality and universality of Western theological traditions and, conversely, the assertion of the importance of paying respect to marginalized ones. This has given credibility to Third World theologies as valid expressions of cultural and political Christian theology. Another consequence has been to alert us to the way in which some dominant theological stances have served the élites and oppressed the underclasses. Though neither of these positions is particularly new, they have probably gained more widespread acceptance since the rise of postmodernism.

Postmodernism is not so much a philosophical position as a loose and diffuse eclectic* cluster of approaches, which are not necessarily self-consistent. It is therefore difficult to refute by rational argumentation – and if it were refuted, postmodernists would counter that such rational argumentation was only an option anyway and one which presumed the possibility of neutral and universal human reason! However, its approach does involve a logical contradiction: in claiming that there is no such thing as a 'grand narrative' (a universally valid position), it is itself asserting a grand narrative by making a judgement which it claims to be universally valid! Furthermore, it needs to be pointed out that to claim that all positions are options (not objective truth) does not at all exclude the possibility that absolute truth exists. Put theologically, while we must admit that we each see God in a different way (as this book argues), this does not mean that God does not exist, only that he is not completely knowable to the human mind. Though our perceptions of God may differ according to our different contexts, and though we can never be completely neutral and objective, we nevertheless as

Christians believe that God does exist objectively and beyond all our incomplete perceptions of him. It is therefore difficult for Christians completely to accept the postmodernist agenda, for the Christian faith is essentially faith in a God who *is* absolute and universal (which in postmodern terms is a 'grand narrative'). At the same time, we have to accept that full and perfect objective knowledge of God is not attainable to human reason.

A related trend which has gained some popularity in recent years is 'postcolonialism'*. Postcolonialism had its origins in modern cultural studies (itself a problematic discipline) and in literary criticism. It is not surprising, therefore, that one of its main influences has been in the field of biblical interpretation. Postcolonialism shares many of the assumptions (and the weaknesses) of postmodernism, but as the term implies it focuses its attention on the colonization by the West of much of the world and the serious results which this has engendered. Another of its themes is that Western literature is 'colonial' in that it presents a pejorative view of non-Western cultures and societies as inferior to those of the West (a claim which was popularized by the use of the term 'orientalism'*). Even the Bible, it is asserted, is used in the interests of colonialism rather than for the liberation of the oppressed.

There is certainly truth in all this (see p. 66), and it is quite clear that no one is completely objective – we all have our presuppositions, however much we may try to overcome them (see p. 28)! However, there are problems with postcolonialism as an over-arching model for interpretation. Strangely, although postcolonialism claims to be representing the views of the 'grass roots' of former colonized societies, many of its leading advocates are élite scholars domiciled in the rich West. Furthermore, the unremitting emphasis on colonialism tends to deflect from the current dire problems of the Third World, many of which are caused as much by political corruption and natural disasters as by postcolonial politics and world economics. Nor does all Western literature (even that produced during the colonial era) have such a jaundiced view of non-Western societies as some postcolonialists would have us believe.

There is perhaps a need for caution here. Postmodernism and post-colonialism (along with the related theories of 'orientalism' and 'multi-culturalism') function as interpretative systems just like ideologies. Like all ideologies they are themselves options, not neutral positions (see p. 28). Our task in doing theology should be to resist being seduced by persuasive rhetoric, and to analyse carefully the assumptions on which various positions are based. Only then can we see how far they are consonant with the values of the Gospel and how far they may, or may not, be used to make the Gospel more meaningful in our own context.

PHILOSOPHY AND THEOLOGY: INDIAN AND AFRICAN EXAMPLES

It is not only Western theology which makes use of a philosophical framework. Some of the earliest attempts at Christian theology in India and Africa did the same thing by attempting to draw on world-views influenced by Indian and African religious concepts.

Bhavani Charan Banerji (1861–1907), who is better known by the name he adopted on his conversion to Christianity, Brahmabandhab Upadhyaya, was one of the first Indian Christians to experiment with transforming the traditional characteristics of Indian religious experience into Christian terms. He adopted the life-style of a sannyasin* (wandering ascetic), set up ashrams* (religious communities) and even underwent the traditional Hindu cleansing ritual (*prayascitta**) to remove the defilement he believed he had acquired through a visit to Britain. He was also deeply involved in the independence struggle.

In his theology Brahmabandhab set himself the task of reconciling Christian thought to the Hindu world-view by making use of the philosophical religious system of Vedanta* and the concept of non-dualism* developed by the Indian sage Sankara. He believed that Christianity must utilize the traditional thinking of the people, and argued that Vedanta could do the same service to the Gospel in India as Greek philosophy did in Europe. 'The truths of the Hindu philosopher', he wrote, 'must be baptized and used as stepping stones to the Catholic faith. The European clothes of the Catholic faith should be laid aside as soon as possible. It must assume the Hindu garment which will make it acceptable to the people of India.' Brahmabandhab developed the Vedanta concept of Absolute Being as *sat* (being), *cit* (consciousness), *ananda* (bliss) to illustrate the Trinity. *Brahma* (God) is Absolute Being, while created beings have no existence in themselves but are dependent upon *Brahma* and share in his being. Knowledge of God (*jñana**) is not simply knowledge of the *Ishvara** of Hinduism (the God who belongs to the world of appearances as we see it, not to 'real' existence) but truly *nirguna Brahma**, God as He is in His essential being. Here is an attempt to use the terminology and the ideas of philosophical Hinduism to convey the essence of the Christian idea of God.

An African philosophy has taken shape only within the last three or four decades. But as long ago as 1945 a Belgian priest working in the then Congo, Placide Tempels, published a book in which it was argued for the first time that African cosmological* thought was systematic and coherent. Tempels' main contention was that the Bantu world-view was dominated by the idea of life-force and that the universe was perceived as a hierarchy of beings which shared to differing degrees in this life-force. At the top of the ladder of power was God Himself, while in the human realm ancestors, chiefs and other humans participated to a lesser extent in life-force, as did the rest of animate and inanimate creation. These forces interacted and were manipulated, the stronger influencing the weaker.

Though Tempels' work has been subjected to a good deal of criticism, it has had a very considerable influence, especially among French-speaking African theologians. Mulago, for example, accepted the ideas of a hierarchy of beings and of life-force, and set out a theology based on what he terms 'vital union'. Both he and others have developed their theology through Tempels' framework.

CHRISTIAN THEOLOGY AND NON-CHRISTIAN RELIGIONS

Philosophy, as we said at the beginning of this chapter, has often had a close relationship with religion, and our last two examples have been taken from philosophies which are reflections of non-Christian religious ideas. How do non-Christian religions affect the task of doing Christian theology, and what is the relationship between Christianity and 'other faiths'?

Christians cannot avoid coming into contact with people of other religions. Even in the Western Christianized world there are large minorities of Jews, Hindus, Muslims, Buddhists and others, as well as those who would claim to be atheists or agnostics. In sub-Saharan Africa as a whole Christians are in a minority – reliable estimates put the Christian population at about 30%. In Asia, overall, Christians are only about 3%, and in some countries less than 1% (the main exception is the Philippines with about 98% Christian, but Korea and Singapore also have substantial Christian minorities). Asian religions, like Hinduism and Buddhism, tend to be more tolerant of other faiths than does Islam. Oceania and Latin America, despite their dominant Christian populations, have many adherents of primal religions. Christian theology, then, is obliged to consider these alternative religious experiences and spiritualities very seriously, and the question of the relationship between Christianity and other faiths is a very important one.

THE EXCLUSIVIST POSITION

One strand of Christian thinking has attempted to answer this problem simply by denying the validity of other religions. This can be called the exclusivist* approach, since it effectively excludes all non-Christian religions from any part in divine revelation. The Christian faith, so this argument goes, claims to be ultimate – there is no way to God except through Christ. Therefore all other religions and claims to salvation must be false, misguided or simply satanic. Many conservative Christians would adopt this position, and it played a powerful role in the impetus for Christian missions during the eighteenth and nineteenth centuries.

Now it would not be difficult for committed Christians to point out some of the more obvious moral problems with regard to non-Christian faiths, which seem to be incompatible with the idea of a loving God – caste in Hinduism, for example, or *Jihad** or the treatment of women in some forms of Islam. These things cannot be explained away as aberrations, for they are justified in the sacred writings of these faiths. (By the same token non-Christians could no doubt point out equally serious moral shortcomings in the history of Christianity, though it would, I believe, be hard to show that they are countenanced in the New Testament.) The exclusivist position is therefore not so easily dismissed.

The neo-orthodox theologian Karl Barth has presented this position with rather more theological sophistication. For him all 'religion' was false, since he regarded it as a human activity which contradicted the initiative of God in revelation. Revelation, in his view, is the sovereign God breaking into human experience through His word. It comes 'vertically' from above, from God alone. This revelation, argued Barth, could take place only through Jesus Christ. All claims to the knowledge of God outside Christ were false. On this view there is no theological significance in non-Christian faiths except as a demonstration of human sinfulness and ignorance and of the futility of the human search after God.

The exclusivist position raises many important questions. Here I shall mention only two. If it is accepted, then we shall also logically have to reject the idea of 'general revelation'*, that is, that God shows Himself in some measure to all peoples everywhere. This concept, though, is one which is generally accepted by Christian theology and indeed (as we have noted) finds its justification in the Bible itself. It would therefore be somewhat drastic to abandon it in the interests of denying some sort of validity to other faiths.

Barth's position, that revelation can take place only through Christ, also raises the problem of revelation in the Old Testament. Barth himself sees the Old Testament also as revelation in Christ. This is not a very easy position to maintain, but if it is accepted we could equally well argue that other non- or pre-Christian religions also partake of the same kind of 'revelation in Christ'.

A second problem with the exclusivist view is that it does not really ring true to most people's experience. No one who has had experience of genuine spirituality in non-Christians or those of non-Christian faiths will find it easy to hold confidently to the exclusivist position.

A less extreme, but ultimately equally exclusivist, view has been to claim that all that is good and true in non-Christian religious experience ultimately derives from Christ. The early Greek Fathers, as we have seen, saw Christ as the *Logos* which is the enlightening principle in all religious philosophies and is behind all religious truth. Thus they understood all that is positive in them to be ultimately 'Christian'.

A more subtle form of this view has been propounded by the Roman Catholic theologian Karl Rahner. According to him we can regard the sincere believer in pre-Christian religions as an 'anonymous Christian', or a 'Christian in the making'. But Rahner's position seems to have the appearance of theological and cultural neo-colonialism! In claiming for Christianity all that is good in other religions, it fails to consider them in their own right. But if their claims are to be taken seriously and if they are to be honestly assessed this is precisely what we have to do.

THE INCLUSIVIST* POSITION

At the other end of the scale are those who want to be all-inclusive, and who are very anxious to acknowledge not only the good in non-Christian religions, but also to argue that they are 'true' for salvation. John Hick, in his many writings, has developed the idea of a 'Copernican revolution'* of faiths, by which he argues that all religions are valid for salvation. He writes: 'The great religious traditions represent different human perceptions of and responses to the same infinite divine Reality.' So instead of thinking of the different claims of the world's religions as mutually exclusive, they should be seen as a kind of continuum, a continuous whole, not true or false, but different cultural and historical expressions of knowledge of the one God.

Though Hick has to recognize, of course, that there are conflicts between different religions and their teaching, he takes the optimistic view that if we wait long enough they will come to grow together, and the various religions will come to be seen as but different options in the approach to God, much in the same way as the different Christian denominations are today. This approach has a lot in common with the classical Hindu concept that there are many different ways to approach the one Absolute. Hick assumes that the world is developing in a dialectical fashion into one great happy family of religions.

However, the modern world, with all its conflicts – and especially its religious ones – gives very little encouragement for this kind of scheme. Clearly we shall have to wait a very long time to see whether Hick is right or not, and in the mean time Christian theologians will have to struggle to find a more immediately relevant approach to non-Christian faiths in the world as it is now.

Respect for other people's faiths and the values we perceive in them does not, of course, necessarily mean accepting them as 'true' or even as alternative ways of salvation (however we understand this word, and it is clear that it means different things in different religions). Conflict between the various world faiths also raises the question of whether it is reasonable to believe in a God who would choose to reveal Himself in ways which seem to human beings to be mutually exclusive. In fact the 'inclusive' view of religions can be just as dogmatic as the 'exclusivist' one, if it claims a monopoly of the truth about religions and to have the ultimate answer to all religious quest.

Many Christians (and no doubt many adherents of other religions as well) will probably feel that to accept the slogan that 'all religions are true' and are simply different ways of approaching the same God is seriously to call into question the whole idea of religious commitment. If I am not convinced that my faith embodies in some way a fuller knowledge and experience of God, which is not available in the same way to adherents of other faiths, then it might be more reasonable and honest for me to cease to be religious altogether. More logically perhaps, I might become a Hindu, a religion which does believe in the validity of all religions as a way to God.

MEDIATING POSITIONS

If the exclusivist and inclusivist approaches to non-Christian religions do not really give us a satisfactory solution, then we shall probably have to look for a mediating position of some kind. Here I shall not presume to propound an answer to the problem, but simply suggest three broad positions which have been adopted by Third World theologians. I then leave readers to evaluate them in the light of their own experience.

The first regards non-Christian religions as a *praeparatio evangelii**, a preparation for the Gospel. On this view the function of non-Christian religions is to expose the problems of the human situation, our sinfulness, our alienation from God and from our own humanity. It creates a sense of need, a felt awareness of God which can only ultimately be fulfilled by revelation through the preaching of the Gospel.

On this view the role of religions is less positive than diagnostic: it diagnoses and exposes the human need. Revelation in other religions is not so much revelation of the nature and purposes of God as revelation of our own existential situation. We may perhaps ask whether this approach gives enough space for accepting the positive religious values of non-Christian religions. It seems to lean towards the exclusivist position.

A more radical approach has been to assert that non-Christian faiths (or at least some of them) really do have a genuine saving value. African scholars like John Kibicho and Gabriel Setiloane have argued that African religions had power for salvation and that God was genuinely known in pre-Christian Africa. A similar position has been taken up by some Indian Christians. This view does indeed take non-Christian faiths very seriously. However, it faces us with the problem of the inclusivist approach: if God was fully known before the acceptance of Christianity, then what, if anything, does Christianity add to revelation? Apparently it cannot be anything essential to salvation, if this was fully recognized before the advent of the Gospel.

A somewhat different method has been employed by several Indian theologians with regard to Hinduism. They have understood Hinduism not so much in terms of a religion but rather in terms of a culture. Brahmabandhab, to whom we referred earlier in this chapter, believed it was possible to be a Hindu and a Christian at the same time. The Indian Christian, he thought, could accept 'cultural' Hinduism without accepting Hinduism as religious truth, for culture belongs to society whereas religion belongs to the sphere of the individual.

It is true that in many societies – and not only in India – religion and culture are so closely intertwined as to make an exact separation of the two very difficult. This is especially the case with rituals like rites of passage. Initiation ceremonies, for instance, though they are properly religious, also admit the novice into full membership of the tribe or society.

On the other hand, conversion from one religion to another will usually involve personal or imposed decisions as to which practices of the old religion are contrary to the new, which are to fall away and which may be retained or transformed. Brahmabandhab probably went too far in regarding Hinduism as a whole as social rather than religious, but he pointed to a very important factor which this book has sought to stress, namely that Christianity in the non-Western world can never be content simply to take over Western Christian theology and practice. It has the obligation continually to examine, to criticize and to transform received forms in conformity with its own cultural heritage.

The issue of the relationship of Christian revelation to non-Christian religions is a delicate and complex one. On the one hand, few of us who have come to the Christian faith from another religion (even at two or three generations' distance) would want, or indeed be able, to deny that those religious traditions do contain a genuine knowledge of God and do produce genuine spiritualities. On the other hand, as Christians, there is within us a conviction that the ultimate salvific* revelation of

God to man is found in Jesus Christ. These two facts, apparently contradictions, must provide a groundwork for a theological approach to non-Christian religions.

However, it ought to be clear that what the theologian is talking about at this point is revelation or knowledge of God, and that this is not the same thing as human salvation. To argue that Jesus Christ is God's ultimate revelation to humankind does not commit us to believing that all but Christians are eternally damned. God's redemption cannot be limited by our human understanding.

It is interesting that the old Jewish rabbis (who are often wrongly accused of wanting to exclude all Gentiles from salvation) believed that 'righteous Gentiles' who kept what they called the 'precepts of Noah' (the basic moral principles given by God to human beings at the beginning of creation) were also God's fellow-workers and shared in His grace. Perhaps this has something to teach us as Christians in our approach to those who do not share our faith.

STUDY SUGGESTIONS

WORDS AND MEANINGS

1 What is the difference between philosophy and religion?
2 Briefly define:
   (a) the 'Absolute';
   (b) hellenism;
   (c) exclusivism;
   (d) universals;
   (e) inclusivism;
   (f) ashrams.
3 Explain what is meant by:
   (a) *praeparatio evangelii*;
   (b) salvific;
   (c) patristic;
   (d) a philosophical vacuum.

REVIEW OF CONTENT

4 What direct influence did Greek philosophy have on the Greek church Fathers?
5 Give an outline of the ideas underlying:
   (a) Existentialism, and
   (b) Marxism, and show how each contributed to the development of modern theology.
6 In what ways did the Indian Christian Brahmabandhab attempt to reconcile Christian thought to the Hindu world-view?

STUDY SUGGESTIONS

7 Give an outline of the idea which according to Placide Tempels has dominated the Bantu (African) world-view, and has strongly influenced the work of African Christian theologians. (If you can, read the book *Bantu Philosophy* by Tempels listed on p. 106 before answering this question.)

CONTEXTUAL APPLICATION AND DISCUSSION

8 What philosophies, if any, are there in your own culture which can be used as stepping-stones or vehicles for Christian theology?
9 How can we distinguish between religion and culture? In what ways, if any, can other religions be utilized in doing Christian theology?
10 What are the advantages and disadvantages of the inclusivist approach to other faiths?
11 Is the idea of 'anonymous Christians' a valid one? If not, how can we deal theologically with sincere believers in other faiths?
12 What problems arise for Christian believers from the view that all religions lead to salvation?

9
The Challenge of Doing Theology

BIBLICAL THEOLOGY AND HISTORICAL THEOLOGY

In the foregoing chapters I have used the word 'theology' in a general and rather inclusive way. Theologians, however, have traditionally distinguished between what they term 'biblical theology'*, 'historical theology'* and 'systematic theology'*. The problems associated with the last of these will be looked at in this section. But first it will be helpful to attempt briefly to define these branches of theology more closely.

The term 'biblical theology' can be used in two ways. Sometimes it is used simply to mean those theologies which claim to be based on the Bible. More technically, however, it describes a trend in nineteenth- and twentieth-century theology which attempted to interpret the biblical books in terms of their own world and background (we have largely followed this approach in chapter 2). To do this it engaged in the detailed study of biblical languages and also took seriously the chronological development of religious and theological ideas during the biblical period. One particular problem this approach highlighted was that of the relationship between the two Testaments, and in practice most of the studies on biblical theology have concentrated on the theology of either the Old or New Testaments.

Historical theology gives an account of the development of Christian thought from apostolic times to the present day. Its method often takes a particular doctrine, say christology or ecclesiology*, and tries to show how it has been understood in different periods of the Church's history. In a sense both biblical theology and historical theology are a search for information – finding out what other people have said, whether the biblical writers or the Christian theologians of the past – rather than creatively 'doing' theology, and both make use of critical linguistic and historical methods. Though, as we have stressed earlier, no one can be completely 'neutral' in dealing with the sources, biblical and historical theologians have to strive as far as possible to lay aside their own religious convictions in order to get at the material of the Bible and Christian history as objectively as possible.

We have seen in chapters 3 and 4 that the task of doing theology involves making use of the findings of both biblical and historical theology. Theologians have to examine the roots of Christian belief as set out in the Bible and they have also to dialogue with great Christian

SYSTEMATIC THEOLOGY

thinkers of the past. But, as we have suggested (p. 39), neither the Bible nor past Christian history can speak directly to us today. They provide us with the basis, the raw materials on which a relevant theology for our own time and situation can be elaborated in our own cultural and social setting.

SYSTEMATIC THEOLOGY

A DEFINITION

In speaking of 'theology' we may mean a particular doctrine, one aspect of Christian truth like, say, the doctrine of Christ or of the sacraments. However, the word 'theology' is more usually understood to imply a coherent elaboration of Christian teaching as a whole. This is usually called 'systematic theology' or 'dogmatics'*. Systematic theology seeks to express Christian truth in a methodical way; it tries to relate particular doctrines to each other so that they are self-consistent and make up a coherent unity. The rationale* behind this exercise is the need to check whether the different affirmations that we make at various times and in various contexts are mutually consistent. It is also (as we have argued in chapters 5 to 8) so that we can relate this whole system of Christian belief to other areas of human life and other ways of expressing the totality of human experience and knowledge.

SOME DIFFICULTIES

Now there are some serious problems involved in this procedure. It has been suggested, for example, that the idea of systematic knowedge is a Greek concept and not a specifically biblical one, and that therefore the very exercise of systematic theology has a philosophical rather than a Christian rationale. This may well be true. However, what is really in question here is not the historical origin of the idea of 'systems' but whether it is a valid one to apply to Christian thought.

A more serious objection, perhaps, is the argument that God is too big to be enclosed in any system formulated by the finite human mind. There is, as we have shown, an unknowableness about God which defies definition. As Terstegen once remarked, 'a God fully comprehended is no God'. This kind of approach lies behind mysticism* – the conviction that God can only be fully known by felt experience and not by intellectual reflection.

At best, therefore, on this view, systematic theology must always be tentative and partial knowledge, and it can never be a complete system of the knowledge of God. In fact most systematic theologians have recognized this and have willingly acknowledged that their systems are never complete or final. Even Karl Barth remarked that his *Church*

Dogmatics was offered 'not as a conclusion, but the initiation of a new exchange of views about the question of a proper theology'.

Others have questioned whether systematic theology is either legitimate or possible, even on the basis of the biblical sources. Even a cursory examination of the Bible indicates that there are different formulations given of particular ideas – 'doctrines', to use our later term. John's christology, for example, is significantly different from that of Mark; Paul's account of the eucharist in 1 Corinthians seems to have little relation to the accounts of the common meal in the Book of Acts. There are even points at which the same author seems to give differing views about the same topic – Paul's eschatology, for example, appears to have modified during his lifetime. And some important aspects of Christian doctrine have a very limited basis in the New Testament – Pentecost and the ascension of Christ are found only in Acts, the virgin birth only in Matthew and Luke.

Now it may be true that some of these apparent differences are simply differences of emphasis rather than of fact; but (so the objection runs) they give the uncomfortable impression that a 'systematic' theology may be trying to force diverse sources into an inappropriate straitjacket which does not allow each source to speak for itself. And it is clear enough that not a few of the older attempts at systematizing doctrine – both conservative as well as liberal, Protestant as well as Catholic – do resort to special pleading and a misuse of biblical texts in order to formulate systems which are fully and neatly coherent and logical.

So again there is much force in this argument; it serves to warn us that one task of systematic theology has to be honestly to expose the tensions in different biblical and historical sources. This would lead us to see its task as that of creating a dialogue between the theologians and their sources, and also between the sources themselves. The conclusions of systematic theology will thus be seen as tentative and not definitive.

Systematic theologians may, on the other hand, respond that there certainly is a broad unifying factor in Christian theology, which is also the unifying factor in the diverse documents of the New Testament, namely the saving event of Jesus Christ. Ebeling quite rightly remarks that 'theology is an indispensable whole because it has to do with one single, fundamentally simple, "Word of God" or "the event of the Word of God"', by which he means the saving revelation in Jesus Christ. It is this event, then, which is the focus and the unifying factor of all Christian thought.

This does not of course mean that all biblical texts can be neatly accommodated, and it will be only honest to confess that there are some points at which systematization is frankly impossible. Probably the most notorious of these areas is eschatology. But at the same time it ought to be possible to give a reasonable account of the faith which we have, and therefore to formulate a broad system of Christian belief which is both coherent and self-consistent. However, we shall also have to acknowledge that both because our sources are in places problematic and because our own understanding of God is incomplete, there will inevitably be some pieces of the jigsaw which cannot neatly be fitted in.

A further problem with systematic theology is a more philosophical one. It is that 'systematic theology' is by definition 'static'. Revelation, if we have correctly discerned it, in the Christian sense is essentially an historical process; it does not drop down from heaven as logical propositional* statements. Systematic theology, on the other hand, is not a dynamic movement. It seeks to state the Christian truth for a particular time and place, and to do this it has no option but to use propositional statements. It takes a 'still-life' picture, a single photograph of what is essentially a moving film. It can therefore only be an approximation to our primary sources of revelation, since it reduces what is 'diachronic', belonging to different times or periods, to something 'synchronic', belonging to the same time or period.

Further, because any systematic theology is formulated at a specific time and in a specific context, it will always be historically and situationally conditioned. While it will hopefully have characteristics which are of enduring value, it can never reasonably be accepted unchanged and unmodified either by future generations or by those elsewhere in the Christian world. In this respect the great systems of the past will require constant re-writing and 'updating' – as, for example, Barth attempted to do with the theology of the Reformers.

Clearly to attempt to reimpose on the present-day Church unmodified any theological system of the past, however venerable, whether that of Augustine, Aquinas, Calvin or whoever, is to fail to recognize that an analysis of our present situation is an essential ingredient to doing theology. Theology has to be 'done', not regurgitated. This is to acknowledge (in Wiles' phrase) 'the continually changing and essentially temporary nature of the theological task'.

A final problem is one that we have referred to earlier. There we noted that everyone who does theology cannot avoid doing so from a particular standpoint and tradition, and usually from within a particular Church tradition. A systematic theology, to a greater or lesser extent, reflects the theologian's own confessional base. It will be recognizably Catholic, Reformed, Orthodox or whatever. This fact also reminds us that all theology is a human activity, albeit done under the guidance of the Spirit of God. Our attempts to express our faith systematically and coherently, to 'justify the ways of God to man', will always be hesitant and stumbling, incomplete and fallible. It is therefore a task to be taken on with humility. As Barth once commented, final authority belongs to God and not to systems of theology.

Systematic theologians have not always understood their task in this way. Before the eighteenth-century intellectual movement known as the Enlightenment, both Catholic and Reformed theologians in the main saw their task as one of using the sources of Scripture, tradition and reason to demonstrate the correctness of their own Church's dogmas over against those of others. Systematic theology, in other words, sought to demonstrate its own ecclesiastical orthodoxy and to expose what it saw as false in other traditions. This method was 'deductive'. Taking their presuppositions from Scripture and tradition theologians regarded it as possible by the exercise of reason to deduce true doctrine from these authoritative sources.

It was during this period that traditional 'divisions' of systematic theology were refined – theology proper (the doctrine of God), christology (doctrine of Christ), soteriology (the doctrine of salvation), ecclesiology (the doctrine of the Church), eschatology (the doctrine of the last things). This terminology, though not so much the same rigid divisions, remains with us today.

The Enlightenment's questioning of tradition and emphasis on reason and science and belief in human progress drastically shook these foundations, at least outside of Roman Catholicism. It showed that no authority and no dogma could simply be taken for granted any more. Perceptions as to the task of systematic theology were therefore modified. Schleiermacher, for example, understood dogmatics as simply the reflection of the state of Christian teaching within a particular Church at a particular time, a kind of relativist viewpoint which fitted in well with his emphasis on subjectivity as characteristic of religion.

Other nineteenth-century theologians saw their task as primarily apologetic. They sought to demonstrate from reason and 'natural theology' the nature of religion in general and then to show that Christianity best fitted this pattern. While both approaches proved inadequate, the two strands of 'ecclesiastical' and 'apologetic' theology remain with us today. Among modern reconstructions Barth's *Church Dogmatics* explicitly reflects the one and Tillich's *Systematic Theology* the other.

Post-Enlightenment theology may be characterized as empirical rather than deductive. It takes the role of the personal much more seriously, in that the spiritual experiences both of the individual believers and of the whole Church are seen as part and parcel of the data of theology. Theology thus becomes a kind of verbalization of Christian experience in the light of Scripture and tradition. So theology is not simply an intellectual affair: commitment and emotion, ethics and worship also have a role to play. Put another way, the Holy Spirit both inspires the Christian experiences which form part of the data of theology and guides the process of doing theology.

What then is the relationship between systematic theology today and its roots in biblical and historical theology? Various models have been suggested. One is that the task of modern systematic theology is simply to 'draw out' or unfold what is already there in the biblical sources – like the flower unfolding in the sunlight. Another is that dogma develops by a process of growth – the picture here is of the mature plant emerging from the seed. Both models have their obvious drawback, not least in that the history of doctrine has seldom been all healthy growth and progress.

A more useful model was suggested by Maurice Wiles, who saw theology in terms of what he called 'new ways of looking, new frames of reference, or a change through an alteration of perspectives'. Just as the same face takes on enhanced and different emphases when seen from different angles, so different theologians perceive doctrine from different, but equally valid, points of view. If we extend this metaphor to take in the fact that the owner of the face also grows older as it is perceived, we shall further incorporate into this model the important element of the changes in systematic theology through altered time perspectives.

This idea of 'changed perspectives' in one sense brings us back to the several examples of theologies from Africa and Asia to which we have referred in this book. Some of the most influential of these theologies, as we have seen, have used secular ideologies as the 'epistemological* lens' for new perspectives on Christian theology, and have on this basis not simply reinterpreted specific aspects of doctrine (like christology) but have advocated a radical reorientation of Christian theology as a whole.

Black theology in America took the situation of Black Americans as its new perspective, and tried to encompass the whole theological task from that angle. Liberation theology in Latin America, on the other hand, was (initially at least) not concerned with race but with poverty and oppression. It sought to see theology from the perspective of the 'option for the poor' and to read Scripture from the under-side, that is, from the point of view of those who were powerless and on the margins of society. Feminist theology, as we have seen, takes as its perspective the marginalization of women in a Church and in a theology which it sees as dominated by patriarchalism*.

As we have suggested above, such new ways of perceiving Scripture and the world in which we live have a real contribution to make in causing us to question our own positions and compelling us to examine the validity of our own perspectives. We shall probably have to admit in the light of these movements that we are seldom as 'neutral' and impartial as we think we are, and our approaches to theology will be recognized as being influenced by our race, sex, education, and our social, political and ecclesiastical assumptions. In that respect new perspectives on theology are a continuing challenge. Part of the task of doing theology is to seek answers to the divergent claims with which openness to differing theological perspectives presents us. In our final section we shall examine in a little more detail this problem of 'creative tension' in doing theology.

CREATIVE TENSION IN DOING THEOLOGY

At the end of chapter 2 we suggested that theology revolves around two poles. On the one hand there is the pole of Christian tradition, on the other the context within which the theologian works. Chapters 3 and 4 explored the first pole – the sources of Christian tradition as received in the Bible, the Church's foundation document, and the history of the ways in which Christian thinkers have done theology in the past. Chapters 5 to 8 looked at the main factors which go to make up the second – the context which shapes the theologian's world: culture, society, history, philosophies and religions. As we noted above, the relative importance given to these poles will vary from one theologian to another.

So too will the 'end from which we start', that is, whether we begin to work out our theology from the Bible and then seek to relate this to the context, or whether we begin by analysing our context and work back from there to the sources of tradition. Almost always there will be a tension of some kind between the pole of Christian tradition and the pole of context. Theologians will move into orbit, as it were, in varying degrees and at different times, closer to one pole than the other, as they put more weight on the Scriptures and the historical traditions of their particular Church on the one hand, or on the cultural and socio-political context on the other.

In this final section, and by way of summarizing the preceding pages, I shall try to explore this 'orbital tension' a little further in terms of some of the paradoxes or dichotomies* which influence the way theologians address their task.

THE HUMAN AND THE DIVINE

Perhaps most obviously, theology faces the paradox of the tension between the human and the divine. It claims to take as its subject the supra-empirical – God, His revelation, His ultimate purposes. But at the same time God's revelation does not come to us objectively and directly. In Scripture God (as Calvin once put it) 'stammers out His word' in human speech and through fallible human instruments. The Word of God is filtered through human prophets, sages or apostles, with all their fallibility and propensity to error and sin. It is, again, received by imperfect human agents, for we who perceive it also share in fallible human nature. And when that Word is proclaimed this has to be done through the inadequate medium of human languages, subject as they are to misunderstandings and falsification. God's acts in history, similarly, are 'described' in the Bible, but often in such a way that it is difficult to reconstruct exactly 'what happened', and those events are interpreted, again, by fallible human agents.

At all points – in its origins, interpretation, reception and communication – we have a divine Word which is mediated in human form. Theology cannot avoid grappling with this divine–human paradox. It has to attempt to answer questions such as: How can God reveal Himself to mankind? How can revelation be received? How can the Word of God be communicated in human speech?

Indeed in a sense all Christian doctrine is an attempt to 'close the gap' or overcome the dichotomy between the human and the divine. It is scarcely surprising, then, that so much of Christian theology down the centuries has addressed the problem of how the divine and the human could cohere in a single Person, 'true God of true God' yet 'flesh of our flesh'.

THE OBJECTIVE AND THE SUBJECTIVE

The divine–human dichotomy might equally be put in terms of the tension between the objective and the subjective. Earlier Christian theologians took as their point of departure the Greek assumption that God is infinite and absolute Being, who stands over against a finite world, and that this finite world is dependent upon the Absolute and therefore logical and ordered (an idea contained in the basic meaning of the Greek word for world, *cosmos**). The classical proofs for the existence of God could therefore argue from the order of the universe as a whole to the necessity of a divine first cause, or (in the case of the ontological* proof) from the supposed reality of beings to the necessity of Being.

One reason why these theistic proofs are so unconvincing to modern men and women is that we have a radically different approach to reality. Greek metaphysics, which made God and His cosmos the focus of its thought, has been replaced by an approach which puts the human person firmly in the centre. This 'anthropological turning point', as the Jewish existentialist Martin Buber described it, demonstrated that, in Western thought, meaning in the cosmos need no longer be derived from postulating the existence of God; on the contrary, the world receives its meaning for human beings today from the existence of human beings themselves. Put in theological terms (and this standpoint is already present in Augustine) the 'proof' of the existence of God does not come from the external world, it comes from the self-consciousness of the individual person. In other words, God's existence becomes necessary in order adequately to explain human existence. Knowledge of God, on this view, is not derived from what is outside of ourselves and is not, therefore, 'objectively' demonstrable.

So the idealist philosopher Kant could argue that we 'know' an object of belief in quite a different way from the way we 'know' a fact. Faith, according to Kant, cannot be demonstrated by reason. The real evidence for religion is in what Kant called the conscience or moral sense – what Christians would call our spiritual nature. For theology this means that, logically, we cannot know God as He (objectively) is in Himself, but only as we (subjectively) perceive Him (as we suggested in our definition of theology in chapter 1). Since Kant, theologians have on the whole tended towards the view that making sense of things and events (including God) is a subjective matter, that it is 'our' interpretation of the 'data' which we perceive.

Existentialism, as we have seen, pushed this view to the extreme. For Kierkegaard objective reality was meaningless; truth is inwardness and subjectivity, it is 'a leap of faith', and in a sense it does not matter so much what you commit yourself to, for all that is important is the passionate conviction with which you do so. Existentialism had a considerable influence on theology throughout the twentieth century, and it raises in an extreme form the very basic issue of the objective–subjective dichotomy. While Christianity does indeed claim to be a faith of passionate commitment, it is commitment to something which at the same time Christians believe to be 'objectively' true (the reality of God, the events and meaning of salvation history and so on), and which is true not just (subjectively) for the believer, but (objectively) for the whole world.

It is certainly possible, as the history of the Church has shown, for the Church to emphasize objective truth (dogma) at the expense of the subjective dimension (faith); it is equally possible to be so engrossed in subjective spiritual experience that we lose sight of the fundamental facts which form the basis of Christianity. Theology has to hold these objective and subjective aspects in fruitful tension. It should be neither a cold unfeeling orthodoxy which fails to relate to human experience, nor should it be a hazy mysticism which has no identifiable basis beyond that experience.

The tension between the objective (what is) and the subjective (what we perceive it to be) highlights another important problem of theology, that of interpretation or hermeneutics. The German theologian Ritschl made a distinction between what he called judgements of fact and judgements of value. Critical scholars could, he believed, determine the first 'objectively'; individual believers then, on the basis of these objective facts, make subjective judgements of value. In one way, of course, Ritschl was quite right to point out that we all make value judgements on the basis of what we receive as facts. These value judgements are made in theology as in everything else.

But at the same time it is also true that Christians look at reality – these same 'facts' – from a particular point of view, a 'mind-set' of commitment to the truth of the Christian message (we called this 'being within the theological circle'). In an important sense no one (not even the supposedly objective critical scholar) can avoid taking up a particular stance. As we noted earlier, we all see the world through our own eyes, which are the lenses of our individual personality with all its principles and prejudices, understandings and misunderstandings. To this extent, it can be argued, we see only what we want to see, and only with difficulty and some reluctance do we appreciate facts and arguments which go against our chosen viewpoint. In this sense the Christian faith is to some extent similar to an ideology, for it claims to be a truth which embraces and explains all reality.

In another way, however, a Christian theology (ideally at least!) differs from an ideology in that it is both critical of itself and open to other viewpoints. Because they recognize that there is a human and subjective element in doing theology, theologians will acknowledge that no theological position has the monopoly of the truth, and that all such positions stand in need of correction or modification. Theological commitment does not mean a closed mind. My own interpretations and perceptions of God and of revelation can never be absolute and infallible. We might characterize this as a tension between commitment and conviction on the one hand, and openness to views which might lead us to modify our stance on the other.

The objective–subjective tension which we have been discussing in these paragraphs also raises serious issues for theology. Given that there is always a subjective element in knowledge, can we ever know God as He really is? What is the relationship between God 'out there' and God as I perceive Him to be? How can I be sure that my subjective experiences of God are valid and not a delusion? How can we be open to other viewpoints while remaining committed to what we believe is the truth of the Christian faith?

ORTHOPRAXIS AND ORTHODOXY

A tension of a rather different kind has been exposed by the theology of liberation. This, it will be remembered, puts an emphasis upon theology as action, and would prefer to talk of ortho*praxis* rather than ortho*doxy*. Its question is not (as was Bonhoeffer's), 'How can we speak of God to a world which has "come of age"?' – that is, to a generation which feels no need to postulate God in order to explain the world. Liberation theology's question is rather, 'How can we speak of God to people who are exploited, oppressed, in abject poverty, and whose existence is less than human?'

Its answer (in part at least) is that we can 'speak' of God to such people by what we *do*, by liberative action on behalf of the oppressed, that is, by orthopraxis. Action takes precedence over reflection and is prior to it in point of time. This action is itself 'doing theology', though theology will also include subsequent reflection on what has been done. Liberation theologians, would, of course, go on to argue that God is 'in' the liberating action of Christians, which is thus part of saving history.

The theology of liberation has raised in a striking way the relationship between action and faith. It would be untrue to say that liberation theology dismisses the need for personal faith, though it would probably be fair to argue that it generally does not say too much about it. To ask, 'Which comes first, faith or action?' is probably to raise a false question. Christian praxis depends on the level of our commitment, which in turn implies our personal faith, devotion and meditation; but faith which does not issue in liberative action is also, as James reminds us in his Epistle, faith which is dead. Faith and praxis are inseparable, though the emphasis we place on each will be a matter of debate.

IDENTITY AND INVOLVEMENT

Our final tension is one to which we have alluded several times in this book in different ways. It has been described by Jürgen Moltmann as the dilemma between identity and involvement. Moltmann puts it as follows:

> The more theology tries to be relevant to the social crises of its society, the more deeply it is itself drawn into the crisis of its own Christian identity. This two-fold crisis is called the 'identity-involvement dilemma'. But it is not a product of the twentieth century, nor is it in fact a dilemma. It is of the essence of Christian theology from its inception that it investigates ever anew its relevance to the world and its identity in Christ.

In pursuing that investigation we may start by summing up the basic questions we shall need to address:

1. How do we relate the Gospel, accepted to be a truth of universal relevance for all times and for all peoples, to our own very particular time and people?

2. How are we to define the essence of the Gospel, given that it comes

to us in the New Testament in the thought-forms and language of a very specific culture?

3. Since culture itself is dynamic and ever-changing, can theology stay still while culture moves?

4. How do we translate the Gospel into the cultural symbols of our own age and context?

5. What criteria can we use to decide what in our culture and context should be accepted as valid and a vehicle for Christian theology?

These are all variants of what doing Christian theology is surely all about, namely, how the Word of God, which comes to us from a different time, culture, language and context, can become the Word of God for us in our own time and context.

STUDY SUGGESTIONS

WORDS AND MEANINGS

1 Briefly define:
   (a) paradox;
   (b) dichotomy;
   (c) diachronic;
   (d) mysticism;
   (e) idealism;
   (f) ontological.
2 Explain what is meant by:
   (a) a value judgement;
   (b) the anthropological turning-point;
   (c) the leap of faith;
   (d) post-Enlightenment;
   (e) epistemological lens;
   (f) changed perspectives.

REVIEW OF CONTENT

3 What 'paradoxes' are involved in doing theology, according to this chapter?
4 In what ways and to what extent are all religions and all ideologies both liberating and oppressive?

CONTEXTUAL APPLICATION AND DISCUSSION

5 (a)–(e): Consider critically the five questions listed in the last paragraph of this chapter, with particular regard to the culture, language and context of your own Church and country.

Further Reading

CHAPTER 1

An excellent introduction to the problems of theology is Maurice Wiles, *What Is Theology* (OUP 1976, reprinted many times). J. Moltmann, *Theology Today* (SCM 1988), deals with some of the problems of doing theology in the modern context and examines the contributions of Bultmann, Rahner, Tillich and political theology. Tillich's own important (but difficult) approach can be found in the first volume of his *Systematic Theology Today* (Mowbray 1971, reprinted 1983). Kwesi Dickson, *Theology in Africa* (DLT 1984), contains some helpful comments on theology in an African context, and Choan-Seng Song edited a collection of papers under the title *Doing Theology Today* (Madras, CLS, 1976), to which he contributed an article from the Asian perspective.

CHAPTER 2

Many volumes on the philosophy of religion have chapters on the problem of religious language (see e.g. J. Hick, *The Philosophy of Religion* (Prentice-Hall 1983). The most exhaustive treatment is probably still I. T. Ramsey, *Religious Language* (SCM 1957 and many reprints). The controversy surrounding Bultmann's essay *New Testament and Mythology* can be followed in H. Bartsch (ed.), *Kerygma and Myth* (SPCK 1964); see also R. Bultmann, *Jesus Christ and Mythology* (SCM 1960).

CHAPTER 3

There are numerous introductions to the Old and New Testaments, and initial reference could be made to SPCK's TEF (now called International) Study Guides 10 and 24, and to the introductions to the commentaries in the same series. There is a valuable article on biblical interpretation in the *Jerome Biblical Commentary*. On ideological approaches to the Bible see the books by Gutierrez and Mosala listed below. Elisabeth Schüssler Fiorenza's feminist approach may be found in *In Memory of Her*, a feminist reconstruction of Christian origins (SCM Press 1983). There is a useful summary of the development of Asian feminist theology in Chung Hyun Kyung, *The Struggle To Be the Sun Again* (SCM Press 1992).

CHAPTER 4

Good summaries of the history of the Church will be found in TEF (ISG) Guides 5, 8 and 14. For doctrine in the early period the fullest treatment is still probably J. N. D. Kelly, *Early Christian Doctrines* (5th edition, Continuum 1977; paperback 2000) and *Early Christian Creeds* (A. & C. Black 1958). For primary sources consult H. Bettenson, *Documents of the Christian Church* (OUP many editions). The modern period is brilliantly surveyed in H. Cunliffe-Jones, *Christian Theology since 1600* (Duckworth 1970); John Macquarrie, *Twentieth Century Religious Thought* (5th edition, SCM 2001) and David F. Ford (ed.), *The*

FURTHER READING

Modern Theologians: An Introduction to Christian Theology in the Twentieth Century (2nd edition, Blackwell 2001) are also good surveys, and E. J. Tinsley, *Modern Theology* (Epworth 1979), gives a selection of extracts from leading modern theologians. For *Third World Theologies* see the summaries in the book of that title edited by K. C. Abraham (published for the Ecumenical Association of Third World Theologians by Orbis 1990), which also contains some useful bibliographies. Other selections are D. J. Elwood, *Asian Christian Theology* (Westminster 1980), J. C. England, *Living Theology in Asia* (SCM 1981), J. Parratt, *A Reader in African Christian Theology*, and *Readings in Indian Christian Theology* edited by R. S. Sugirthararjah and Cecil Hargreaves (TEF (ISG) 23 and 29, SPCK 1987 and 1993). Students are advised to read the original sources, i.e. the writings mentioned by the theologians themselves, rather than confining themselves to critical studies about them by others. See also J. Parratt (ed.), *An Introduction to Third World Theologies* (CUP 2004).

CHAPTER 5

For Sawyerr's and Fashole-Luke's arguments regarding the ancestors see *Creative Evangelism* (Lutterworth 1968) and 'Ancestor Veneration and the Communion of Saints' in *New Testament Essays for Africa and the World* edited by M. Glasswell and E. Fashole-Luke (SPCK 1974). Nyamiti's ideas are worked out in *Christ as Our Ancestor* (Gweru, Mambo Press, 1984). Benezet Bujo, *Afrikanische Theologie* is now available in English as *African Theology in Its Social Context* (Maryknoll 1992). Robin Boyd, *An Introduction to Indian Christian Theology* (Madras, CLS, 1969), has a good discussion of Appasamy, but reference can also be made to Appasamy's own book *What Is Moksa?* (Madras 1931).

CHAPTER 6

The approaches of South African Black theology can be studied in *Black Theology, the South African Voice* edited by B. Moore (Hurst 1973), A. Boesak, *Black Theology, Black Power* (also published as *Farewell to Innocence*) (Mowbray 1978), Tutu's article cited below (see p. 107), and, for more recent developments, I. Mosala and B. Thlagale (eds.), *The Unquestionable Right To Be Free* (Skottaville, Johannesburg, 1988). An informative collection of essays on *Dalit* theology is M. E. Prabhakar's *Towards a Dalit Theology* (Delhi, SPCK, 1989). Marianne Katoppo's book *Compassionate and Free* was published by the WCC (Geneva 1976). For *Ujamaa* refer to J. Nyerere, *Freedom and Development* (OUP 1973) and for a Catholic approach to *Ujamaa*, C. Mwoleka, *Ujamaa and Christian Communities* (Gaba, Eldoret, 1976). The best collection on *Minjung* theology is *Minjung Theology, People as Subjects of History*, edited by the Commission on Theological Concerns of the Christian Conference of Asia (Orbis 1983). G. Gutierrez, *A Theology of Liberation* (Orbis 1973 and reprinted many times) is the classic statement of Latin American liberation theology, but J. Bonino, *A Theology of Human Hope* (Orbis 1969), is probably a simpler introduction. Of the many books and reports on political and economic issues in the Third World, the Brandt Report (*North and South, a Programme for Survival*, Pan 1980), though now a little dated, is a balanced and very useful survey.

CHAPTER 7

The classic of the 'salvation history' school is O. Cullman, *Christ and Time* (SCM revised issue 1982), while G. von Rad, *Old Testament Theology* (Oliver and Boyd 1962), remains largely unsurpassed. On the problem of the Gospels see G. Stanton, *The Gospels and Jesus* (OUP) and E. P. Saunders, *The Historical Figure of Jesus* (Penguin 1993). C. S. Song's views are set out in his *Third Eye Theology* (Lutterworth 1980). The books by Boesak and the South American liberation theologians are listed under chapter 6.

CHAPTER 8

There are useful studies of the philosophers mentioned in this chapter in the series *Past Masters* (Oxford) and *Modern Masters* (Fontana). The views of Brahmabandhab are discussed in Boyd's book, see chapter 5. Placide Tempels, *Bantu Philosophy* was published by Presence Africaine, Paris in 1959, and the most accessible writing of Mulago is in *Biblical Revelation and African Belief.* Barth's views on religion are presented in his *Church Dogmatics Vol. 2/1* (T. and T. Clark 1966) and Rahner's idea of anonymous Christians in *Theological Investigations Vol. 5* (DLT 1966 and Seabury 1974). A succinct statement of Hick's theories can be found in his *Philosophy of Religion* (see chapter 2). See also K. J. Vanhoozer, *The Cambridge Companion to Postmodern Theology* (CUP 2003).

References

CHAPTER 2
The quotation on p. 18 is from Albert Schweitzer, *The Quest for the Historical Jesus.*

CHAPTER 3
The quotation on p. 24 is taken from E. Käsemann, *New Testament Questions of Today* (SCM Press 1969), and the illustration of 'seeing' on p. 28 is from the letters of the Jewish philosopher Franz Rosenzweig.

CHAPTER 5
The quotation from Tillich comes from the first volume of *Systematic Theology*; that from Dickson is from *Theology in Africa.* The word 'schizophrenia' has been used by Desmond Tutu in 'Black Theology and African Theology', reprinted in ISG 23.

CHAPTER 7
The quotation on p. 74 is from P. Ellingworth and K. Dickson (eds), *Biblical Revelation and African Belief*, and that from Mercy Oduyoye is from her book *Hearing and Knowing* (Orbis 1986). The quotation from M. M. Thomas is from *The Christian Response to the Asian Revolution* (SPCK 1979).

CHAPTER 8
The reference to Kibicho is his 'The Continuity of the African Concept of God into and through Christianity' in *Christianity in Independent Africa*, ed. E. Fashole-Luke and others (1978), and to Setiloane is 'Where Are We in African Theology?' in *African Theology en Route*, ed. K. Appiah-Kubi and S. Torres (Orbis 1976).

CHAPTER 9
The quotation from Moltmann is from 'Christian Theology and Its Problems Today' in *The Experiment Hope* (Fortress 1975).

Glossary

This extended Glossary gives outline definitions of technical and other terms used in this book (asterisked at first appearance), chiefly for the benefit of general readers and for students reading at this level for the first time. Translations of foreign words and phrases used are also listed.

ADAPTATIONISM, or ADAPTIONISM: in cultural theology an approach which seeks to adapt traditional ideas and practices in such a way as to make biblical ideas and practices more real in the local context, and thus to illuminate the Christian faith.

ALLEGORY, ALLEGORICAL: narrative description of a theological truth in terms of a more familiar image or symbol (e.g. Christ as the vine, John 15).

ANATHEMA, ANATHEMATIZED: a Greek term for a person or thing 'set aside' to be either consecrated to a divinity or 'accursed', i.e. devoted to destruction. Used in the early Church to mean Christians excommunicated on account of serious sin or doctrinal error.

APOCALYPTIC: any books or ideas which resemble the Book of Revelation or 'Apocalypse' in claiming to reveal divine secrets about the 'last days' or Coming of God's Kingdom at the end of time.

APOLOGETICS: the defence of Christian belief by argument, against external criticism or different world-views.

APOSTASY: abandonment of one's religious faith or principles; defection from a particular Church.

APOSTOLIC FATHERS: the early disciples and fellow-workers of the Apostles, particularly those who left written works.

ARYAN: a person of northern European, 'Caucasian' descent; or any one of the Indo-Germanic, Indian and Iranian branches of the Indo-European languages.

ASHRAM: in Hinduism, a place of religious retreat and instruction, where a *guru*, or spiritual leader and instructor, lives and teaches.

BHAGAVADGITA: literally 'the song of the Lord'. Sometimes just called the 'Gita'. A dramatic religious poem, the most famous ethical and devotional religious text of popular Hinduism.

GLOSSARY

BHAKTI, BHAKTISM: in Hinduism, loving devotion to God; the approach of faith to God as personal.

BIBLICAL THEOLOGY: theology which claims to be based on the Bible, especially a trend in nineteenth- and twentieth-century theology which tries to interpret the biblical books in terms of their own world and background.

BLACK THEOLOGY: a movement which has arisen in situations where Christian theologians facing racial discrimination have offered theological reflection upon the struggle of black people for justice; for example, in the USA and more particularly in South Africa.

CASTE: an exclusive and hereditary class, especially amongst Hindus; the caste system serves to enforce a rigid social structure.

CATECHETICAL: official church teaching, learned orally or from a book, set out in the form of question and answer.

CATEGORY, CATEGORIES: the sorts of classes in which ideas or information relating to a subject or field of knowledge can be systematically arranged; in philosophy the different modes of being or sorts of concepts used to understand and interpret reality.

CATHOLIC: (a) Churches in communion with the see of Rome, acknowledging the Pope as supreme head, (b) 'universal', worldwide.

CHARISMATIC: used to describe Churches and other religious movements inspired by a belief in such gifts of the Spirit as healing, speaking in tongues, etc.

CLIMACTIC: the most important high point in any work of literature, art, etc., or period of history.

CONSCIENTIZE, CONSCIENTIZATION: to awaken the conscience of oppressed peoples to recognition of their condition and encourage them to assert their self-dignity.

CONSERVATIVE, CONSERVATISM: tending to support the preservation of established or traditionally accepted ideas, customs, theological positions, etc.; opposed to change.

CONTEXT: the particular historical, geographic, cultural, political, social, economic and religious circumstances in which any Church or community is situated.

CONTEXTUALIZATION: the reception and rooting of the Christian Gospel in a particular context: hence the relation of the Gospel to its historical and local circumstances.

GLOSSARY

COPERNICAN REVOLUTION: the new understanding of the nature of the universe brought about by the discoveries and theories of scientists such as Copernicus, which seemed to conflict with a literal interpretation of the Bible.

COSMOS, COSMOLOGICAL: relating to the whole world or universe.

CREED: a concise, formal and authorized statement or 'confession' defining the faith which the Church, or a section of it, comes to regard as true and to be accepted by its members.

CRITICISM: careful examination and judgement of any form of literature in order to understand its meaning. In doing theology, *'biblical'* or *'higher'* criticism means study of the Bible which takes account of its historical, cultural and social background, and the aims of the author. *'Textual'* criticism means study and comparison of existing manuscripts and versions of the Bible, in order to discover as nearly as possible the text as originally written.

CULTURE, CULTURAL: all the formally and informally accepted institutions, customs and traditions, and the common ideas, values and tastes which find expression in the social behaviour of a regional, national or tribal group or society.

DEISM, DEIST: belief in the existence of a supreme Being (God) who is the ultimate source of reality, but not in a divinely revealed religion.

DEMYTHOLOGIZE: to make explicit a truth or belief traditionally veiled or expressed only implicitly in mythological terms.

DIALECTICAL MATERIALISM, *see* MATERIALISM

DIASPORA: from a Greek term meaning 'dispersed', used to describe the Jews living outside Palestine, who normally spoke in Greek.

DICHOTOMY: separation into two parts.

DOCETISM, DOCETIC: the heretical belief characteristic of Gnostic teaching in the second century, that Jesus' human nature and His death were only apparent, not real.

DOGMA: a belief or doctrine laid down by authority. In Christian theology, a doctrine proclaimed by the Church as a divinely revealed truth.

DOGMATICS: dogmatic theology is the coherent and systematic examination and presentation of all major Christian doctrines, undertaken for and within the Church.

DRACONIAN: (here) oppressive and threatening.

GLOSSARY

DUALISM: in philosophy, the view that spirit and matter are two radically independent elements; in theology the doctrine of two distinct principles of good and evil or two divine beings of these characters. NON-DUALISM in Indian thought, is the idea that the spirit and matter are equally a reflection of the Absolute (Brahman).

ECCLESIOLOGY: the doctrine of the Church.

ECLECTIC: borrowing freely from various different sources.

ECUMENICAL, ECUMENISM: worldwide; committed to the cause of cooperation and eventual re-uniting of the Church as a whole.

ELECTION: the choosing or calling by God of particular people or peoples to carry out, by their service and witness, His plan of salvation for the world.

EMPIRICAL, EMPIRICISM: the assumption that truth is to be discovered only by 'scientific' methods or practice based on physical observation, experience or experiment.

ENLIGHTENMENT: philosophical movement in eighteenth-century Europe which stressed tolerance, reason and the encouragement of scientific investigation.

EPICUREANISM: the teaching of the Greek philosopher Epicurus that the pursuit of pleasure is the greatest good.

EPIGNOSIS: a term used by New Testament writers to mean knowledge by experience, apprehended by the heart and will as well as the mind.

EPISTEMOLOGY: the theory and scientific study of knowledge.

ESCHATOLOGY: study relating to the 'last things', i.e. death, judgement, life after death, heaven, hell; relating to the future.

ESCHATON: the 'end', the consummation of all things.

ESOTERIC: secret, meant only for those initiated.

EXCLUSIVISM: an approach adopted by many conservative and fundamentalist Christians who deny the validity of all other religions, and exclude them from any part in divine revelation or claim to salvation.

EXEGESIS: explanation, critical interpretation of a text, drawing out the meaning as intended by the author in its original context.

EXISTENTIALISM, EXISTENTIAL: the idea that human beings cannot be explained or understood in terms of any general or universal system, but only according to each person's individual existence and experience.

GLOSSARY

FUNDAMENTALISM: originally a movement in American Protestantism; now used to mean the belief that the Bible as a whole and in every part is literally true, and its teaching valid, not only in regard to faith and morals, but also as a factual record of the nature and history of the universe.

GENERAL REVELATION: *see* REVELATION.

GNOSTIC, GNOSTICISM: a religious movement of the early Christian centuries, especially emphasizing the *knowledge* of God and of the nature and destiny of humanity, which was believed to have redeeming power.

HELLENISM, HELLENISTIC: the influence of Greek thought and culture.

HERESY: a belief or opinion contrary to the accepted teaching of the Church.

HERMENEUTICS: the explanation and interpretation of the biblical text in relation to our own present-day situation and culture.

HISTORICAL THEOLOGY: study and interpretation of the way in which Christian theology has developed from Apostolic times to the present.

HISTORICITY: historical truth or actuality.

HISTORY, HISTORICAL: relating to the sequence of events as they have occurred in time.

HOMOOUSIOS: a Greek term meaning literally 'of the same substance', used in the Nicene Creed to describe the relationship between God the Father and God the Son.

HUMANISM: any philosophy or teaching which emphasizes the worth and dignity of human beings: a stance marked in the nineteenth and twentieth centuries by rejection of any religious teaching or belief in the supernatural.

HYPOSTASIS: a Greek term used in several ways: in the New Testament to mean substance or underlying reality, and then in the great credal statements to define the essential nature of Christ.

IDEALISM: a term used to classify any philosophical system or position which described perceived external objects in terms of ideas, concepts or mind, rather than physical matter.

IDEAS: images or perceptions of external objects or experiences formed by the mind; any product of intellectual activity.

IDEOLOGY: a body of ideas forming the basis of a particular way of thinking or behaving, or a particular political, economic or social policy.

IMMANENT: close to, pervasive, the universe.

GLOSSARY

INCLUSIVISM: the approach adopted by Christians who acknowledge the good in other religions also, regarding them simply as different cultural and historical responses to the one same divine Being.

INCULTURATION: expression of the Christian faith in terms which a particular society can relate to and 'clothe' with indigenous cultural forms. Often most evident in adapting local forms of liturgy and worship.

INDIGENIZATION: the reception and rooting of the Christian Gospel and the Church which embodies it, in a given concrete locality. Hence expression of the Gospel in terms that are meaningful to the local population, and development of the Church in forms relevant to that situation.

INTERPRET, INTERPRETATION: to explain the meaning of a text, whether in relation to its original context or to the present day.

JUSTIFICATION: the act through which, by God's grace, faithful and repentant Christians are freed from the penalty of sin, and accounted or made righteous.

LIBERALISM: in contrast to conservatism and fundamentalism, liberalism is receptive to the findings of modern science and the humanities in its pursuit of religious 'truth', and to those of historical and textual criticism in its understanding of the Bible.

LIBERATION THEOLOGY: arose in Latin America in the 1960s, but is relevant in many developing countries. Focusing chiefly on ortho*praxis* rather than ortho*doxy*, its aim is the transformation of society and humanization of people suffering injustice and social, political and economic exploitation.

LINGUISTIC PHILOSOPHY: also known as logical positivism: a materialist philosophy based on the assumption that only things which are experienced by the physical senses are truly real.

LITERALISM, LITERALIST: interpretation which follows only the literal form of a text, taking no account of metaphorical, symbolic or mythical language.

LOGICAL POSITIVISM: *see* LINGUISTIC PHILOSOPHY.

MATERIALISM: used to describe a number of different, and mainly atheistic, philosophical and political standpoints, which interpret all life and history in terms of material and economic forces, and deny or dismiss the independent existence of spirit, e.g. the Marxist doctrine of 'dialectical materialism'.

MATERIALIST EXEGESIS: interpretation of all history and literature, including the Bible, from a materialistic point of view.

GLOSSARY

METAPHOR: the use of 'picture-language', as when a word or phrase normally used to mean one thing is used to give a wider meaning to another, e.g. when Jesus referred to Peter as 'this rock'.

METHODOLOGY: the science of method; the logical principles according to which any branch of learning or line of enquiry, either theoretical or practical, is organized and conducted.

MINJUNG THEOLOGY: arose in Korea in the 1970s, during the repressive regime of President Park. Favouring a socialist emphasis, it works for radical social change to alleviate the suffering of urban workers, peasants and students who are politically oppressed.

MULTICULTURALISM: the idea that all cultures are of equal value.

MYSTERY CULTS: religious movements current in the ancient world, usually focusing on a redeemer figure and requiring special initiation rituals for the adherents.

MYSTICISM: in doing theology mysticism refers to the immediate experience of a divine–human relationship, and especially to the experience of oneness with God.

MYTH, MYTHOLOGICAL: a category of narrative expressing in imaginative form a truth, belief or spiritual experience which cannot be adequately expressed by a simple statement of what happened.

NATURAL SCIENCE: *see* SCIENCES.

NATURAL THEOLOGY: traditionally understood as the knowledge about God and His creation which the human intellect can acquire without the help of divine revelation.

NON-DUALISM: *see* DUALISM.

ONTOLOGY, ONTOLOGICAL: study concerning the nature of being or existence.

ORAL THEOLOGY: theology taught and handed down by word of mouth, not in writing.

ORIENTALISM: originally meaning that which concerned Asia; subsequently used in E. Said's book of this name to denote the pejorative representation of these cultures in Western writing (Said is largely concerned with perceptions of Islam).

GLOSSARY

ORTHODOX, or EASTERN ORTHODOX, CHURCHES: the group of national Churches, each with its own head and owing allegiance to the Ecumenical Patriarch of Constantinople, whose refusal to accept the clause 'and the Son' in the Nicene Creed led to the 'great schism' of 1054.

ORTHODOXY: right or accepted forms of teaching.

ORTHOPRAXIS: right forms of action.

PATRIARCHALISM: supporting the dominance of males over females.

PATRISTIC PERIOD: the early centuries of church history, when much of the literature on which Christian doctrine has since been based was being written. 'Patristics' is the study of that literature.

PIVOTAL: in this context describes an event in history which can be seen as a turning point in the lives of individuals or peoples.

PLATONISM: teaching derived from the Greek philosopher Plato, whose study of such subjects as justice and goodness profoundly influenced Christian theologians over many centuries.

PLURALISM: used here to describe situations where a variety of different religions and cultural systems exist side by side.

POSTCOLONIALISM: an approach which focuses on the damaging process of colonialism, and the misrepresentation of colonized cultures, and claims to speak on behalf of those oppressed by this process.

POSTMODERNISM: the position that there are no absolutely valid truths, but that all options are equally valid.

PRAXIS: action, practice as opposed to theory.

PROPOSITIONAL: set out as a series of statements in logical order, as a basis for understanding or action.

PROSOPON: personification, embodiment.

RATIONALE: the rational theory or principle underlying a particular course of action.

RATIONALISM: the view that reason alone can give certain knowledge of the world as it is.

REFORMATION: the period, in the sixteenth century, when attempts to reform the Church in Europe resulted in the separation of the Protestant Churches from the Roman Catholic Church.

GLOSSARY

REFORMED CHURCHES: sometimes used to describe all the Churches accepting the principles of the Reformation, but also more specifically the Calvinist Churches as distinct from the Lutherans.

REVELATION: God's disclosure of Himself to human beings, both in *'general revelation'* as Creator, through the natural world, and in *'special revelation'* as Redeemer through the Gospel and to particular people at particular times and places.

SACRAMENTALIST: attaching particular importance to the spiritual nature of the sacraments.

SACRED HISTORY: events in the history of the world, especially those recorded in the Bible, through which God is believed to have revealed Himself.

SALVIFIC: saving, resulting in salvation.

SCIENCES: the disciplines or subjects of study and learning which are concerned with things or activities that are observable and measurable: the 'social' sciences with such subjects as anthropology, economics, politics, sociology, etc., and the natural sciences with aspects of the world of nature such as chemistry, physics, botany, zoology, etc.

SCHIZOPHRENIA: a disease in which the patient loses touch with reality and sometimes appears to suffer from a divided personality.

SENSE DATA: information received directly through the physical senses of sight, hearing, touch, etc.

SEPTUAGINT: the Greek version of the Old Testament used by Greek-speaking Jews and early Christians, said to have been translated by seventy-two scholars. It contained the Apocrypha as well as the Hebrew Old Testament canon.

SOCIOLOGY, SOCIETAL: the study of societies, relating to societies.

SOTERIOLOGY: the work of salvation through Christ, as seen in the New Testament and in the history of the Church.

STOICS, STOICISM: a Greek religious philosophy of the New Testament period; it taught the existence of a *Logos* or 'world soul' in which every human being shares, and the identification of nature with reason and indifference to immediate pleasures or sufferings.

SUPRA-EMPIRICAL: used to describe a dimension of reality which goes beyond the physical world of the senses.

SYMBOL: an emblem or sign used to represent some other thing or idea, often having an inherent connection with the thing represented, e.g. a flag to represent a particular nation.

SYNTHETIC: in this context, drawing together the parts of anything into a whole.

SYSTEMATIC THEOLOGY: seeks to express Christian teaching in a methodical way, and relate particular doctrines together in a consistent and coherent whole.

TEXTUAL CRITICISM: *see* CRITICISM.

TRANSCENDENT, TRANSCENDENCE: relating to the Absolute, beyond the limitations of ordinary human knowledge or reason.

VATICAN II: the Second Vatican Council held in 1962–5, heralding more open and ecumenical relationships of the Roman Catholic Church with other Churches and with other cultures and religions, celebration of the mass in vernacular languages, and encouraging a more critical approach to biblical studies.

FOREIGN WORDS AND PHRASES

In this section letters in brackets indicate the language each term originates from: (A) Arabic; (G) Greek; (H) Hebrew; (S) Sanskrit; (L) Latin.

Agape: love, in the sense of charity or loving kindness, as distinct from physical or sexual love (G).
Ananda: joy, bliss (S).
Apartheid: segregation and separate development (of races) (Afrikaans).
Ashram: a place of religious retreat and instruction, where a *guru* lives and teaches (S).
Avarna: outcastes, the lowest social class (S).
Avatar: the 'descent' or coming down to earth of a god (S).
Bantu: the name given to a group of peoples in central and southern Africa and the languages they speak.
Bhagavadgita or *Gita*: the 'Song of the Lord'; the most famous religious and ethical text of Hinduism (S).
Bhakti, bhaktism: loving devotion to God; the approach of faith to God as personal (S).
Brahma: in Hindu Scriptures the Supreme Being or World Spirit; God (S).
Cit (sometimes spelt *chit*): knowledge, consciousness (S).
Cosmos: world or universe (G).
Dal: broken or oppressed (H).
Dalit: oppressed, downtrodden; a term used by the outcastes or 'scheduled castes' in India to describe their suffering and exploited condition (S).
Diaspora: the 'dispersed' or scattered Jews living outside Palestine (G).
Dokei moi: literally 'it seems to me', from which the term 'dogma' derives, meaning an opinion or teaching eventually accepted as authoritative (G).
Epignosis: knowledge gained by experience, heart and will as well as mind (G).
Eschaton: the end; used to mean the end of the world (G).
Gnosis: knowledge (G).
Guru: a spiritual leader and teacher (S).

GLOSSARY

Harijans: literally 'people of God'; a term used by Gandhi for people outside the Hindu caste system previously known as 'outcastes' or 'untouchables' (see *Dalit*) (S).

Hesed: (sometimes transliterated as *chesed*): mercy, compassion; translated in the RSV Common Bible as steadfast love (H).

Homoousios: of the same substance (G).

Hypostasis: basic essence, underlying reality of real personal being (G).

Ishvara: in Hinduism, god as he is perceived by humans, not as he is in his real essence (S).

Jahweh, JHWH, the Hebrew name for God (H).

Jihad: in Islam, a holy war (A).

Jñana: knowledge (S).

Karma: literally 'action', hence the moral result of action. In Hindu philosophy the idea that people's actions in one life-cycle determine their fate or destiny in the next (S).

Kerygma: proclamation or preaching, especially the announcement of what God has done in Jesus (G).

Kurios: Lord (G).

Logos: Greek for 'word', meaning both speaking and what is said. In the Bible God's Word means His creating, activating, sustaining and self-revealing communication to human beings, by means of the Law, the Prophets, the Scriptures and the teaching of the Church. But above all the *Logos* is Jesus Christ: God's most perfect expression of Himself (G).

Maya: illusion or appearance: in Hindu philosophy the created universe as distinct from true reality (S).

Minjung: people, the people (Korean).

Mlungu, Mungu or *Modimo*: some of the names used for God, Divinity or Supreme Being in East and Southern Africa.

Négritude: blackness: the name given to a literary movement among black writers in French-speaking West Africa (French).

Nirguna Brahma: literally 'without attributes'; as used of Brahma, God as transcendent and unknowable (S).

Ortho-: right, correct (G).

Pentateuch: the first five books of the Bible (G).

Pistis: faith (G).

Praeparatio evangelii: preparation for the gospel (L).

Prayascitta: in Hinduism a cleansing ritual (S).

Prosopon: personification, embodiment (G).

Proto: first, hence an original, a type (G).

Rig-Veda: first of the 4 Vedas, the Indian scriptures (S).

Sannyasin: an ascetic; Hindu religious mendicant or beggar; 'one who lays aside' (S).

Sat: truth (S).

Shalom: peace (H).

Sola scriptura: by Scripture alone (L).

Sudra: in Hinduism, the lowest of the four main castes (S).

Supra-: above or beyond (L).

Theos: God (G).

Theotokos: bearer of God, Mother of God (G).

Torah: the Hebrew word for 'law', commonly used to mean the first five books of the Old Testament (H).
Ujamaa: a Swahili word meaning family or kinship, 'togetherness', the concept which Tanzania's 'African Socialism' claimed to be the basis of its policy.
Upanishads: ancient Sanskrit theosophical and philosophical writings; the second group of the Hindu scriptures (S).
Varna: colour, caste (S).
Veda(s): derived from a word meaning 'knowledge', the name given to the four earliest groups of Hindu scriptures, and in general to the whole body of Scripture (S).
Vedanta (see Veda(s)): literally 'the end of the Vedas'. The term is used to describe the essential philosophy of the Upanishads, especially as regards the nature of the Absolute, the soul, and the world (S).
Weltanschauung: world-view; a general way of looking at, or idea about, the nature and purpose of the world (German).

NAMES

Achebe, Chinua (contemporary Nigerian novelist and writer)
Anselm (1093–1109, medieval theologian and Archbishop of Canterbury)
Appasamy, Aiyadurai Jesudason (1891–1975, South Indian bishop and theologian)
Aquinas, Thomas (1225–74, scholastic theologian)
Aristotle (4th century BC Greek philosopher)
Augustine (354–430, Latin theologian and Bishop of Hippo)
Barth, Karl (1886–1968, Swiss Reformed theologian)
Boesak, Allan (contemporary South African theologian)
Bonhoeffer, Dietrich (1906–45, German theologian)
Brahmabandhab Upadhyaya (Bhavani Charan Banerji, 1861–1907, Bengali theologian and nationalist)
Buber, Martin (1878–1965, Jewish existentialist philosopher)
Bujo, Benezet (contemporary Catholic Zairean theologian)
Bultmann, Rudolf (1884–1976, German theologian and New Testament scholar)
Buthelezi, Manas (contemporary South African Lutheran bishop and theologian)
Calvin, John (1509–64, French Reformed theologian)
Darwin, Charles (1809–82, British naturalist, discoverer of natural selection)
Dickson, Kwesi (contemporary Ghanaian theologian)
Dostoievsky, Fedor (1821–81, Russian novelist)
Ebeling, Gerhard (contemporary German theologian)
Fashole-Luke, Edward (contemporary Sierra Leonean theologian)
Fiorenza, Elisabeth Schüssler (contemporary American feminist theologian)
Gandhi, Mohandas (1889–1948, Indian nationalist leader)
Heidegger, Martin (1889–1976, German existentialist philosopher)
Hick, John (contemporary British philosopher of religion)
Hegel, Georg W. F. (1770–1831, German idealist philosopher)
Hume, David (1711–76, Scottish empiricist philosopher)
Katoppo, Marianne (contemporary Indonesian woman theologian)

GLOSSARY

Kant, Immanuel (1724–1804, German rationalist philosopher)
Kaunda, Kenneth (first president of Zambia)
Kibicho, John (contemporary Kenyan theologian)
Kierkegaard, Søren (1813–55, Danish philosopher and theologian)
Luther, Martin (1483–1540, founder of the German Reformation)
Malinowski, Bronislaw (1884–1942, Polish anthropologist)
Marx, Karl (1818–83, German political philosopher)
Moltmann, Jürgen (contemporary German theologian)
Mosala, Itumeleng (contemporary South African theologian)
Mulago gwa Cikala (contemporary Catholic Zairean theologian)
Nehru, Jawahalal (1889–1964, first prime minister of India)
Nestorius (died c.451, Bishop of Constantinople)
Ngugi wa Thiongo (contemporary Kenyan novelist and dramatist)
Nkrumah, Kwame (1909–72, first prime minister of Ghana)
Nyerere, Julius (1922–99, first president of Tanzania)
Nyamiti, Charles (contemporary Catholic Tanzanian theologian)
Oduyoye, Mercy Amba (contemporary Ghanaian theologian)
Oket p'Bitek (Ugandan poet and writer)
Origen (died 253, hellenistic Christian theologian)
Philo, Judaeus (born in Alexandria c.20 BC, hellenistic Jewish philosopher)
Plato (5th century BC, Greek philosopher)
Plotinus (205–70, philosopher, founder of Neoplatonism)
Rahner, Karl (1904–84, German Catholic theologian)
Ramakrishna (1836–86, Hindu ascetic and reformer)
Ritschl, Albrecht (1822–89, German Lutheran theologian)
Sankara (c.700, Hindu religious philosopher)
Sartre, Jean-Paul (1905–80, French existentialist philosopher and writer)
Sawyerr, Harry (1909–87, Sierra Leonean theologian)
Schleiermacher, Friedrich (1768–1834, German liberal theologian)
Sen, Keshav Chandra (1838–84, Bengali Hindu reformer)
Senghor, Leopold (1906–2001, first president of Senegal)
Setiloane, Gabriel (died 2004, South African theologian)
Song, C. S. (contemporary Taiwanese-American theologian)
Tagore, Rabindranath (1861–1941, Bengali poet and writer)
Tempels, Placide (Belgian priest and missionary in Zaire before independence)
Tertullian (died 223, North African Latin theologian)
Thlagale, Buti (contemporary South African priest and theologian)
Thomas, M. M. (contemporary South Indian theologian)
Tillich, Paul (1886–1965, German-American Protestant theologian)
Tolstoi, Leo (1828–1910, Russian novelist and reformer)
Toynbee, Arnold (1889–1975, British historian)
Trevelyan, George M. (1876–1962, British historian)
Tutu, Desmond (contemporary South African archbishop and theologian)
Vivekananda, Swami (1862–1902, Hindu teacher and successor to
    Ramakrishna)
Wiles, Maurice (1923–2005, British theologian)

Key to Study Suggestions

Chapter 1: Getting Started (Pages 1–10)
1. (a) (i), (ii) and (iii) See p. 1.
   (b) See p. 1 (bottom).
2. (a) See p. 2, para. 2.
   (b) See p. 1, para. 2.
   (c) See p. 4, para. 3.
   (d) See p. 9, para. 4.
3. (a) See p. 1, para. 1.
   (b) See p. 4 (bottom).
   (c) See p. 8, para. 3.
   (d) See p. 10, para. 2.
4. See p. 2.
5. See p. 1 (bottom).
6. See p. 3 (top).
7. See p. 8 (top).
8. See p. 5.
9. See p. 9.

Chapter 2: The Language and Context of Theology (Pages 13–21)
1. (a) See p. 13 (bottom).
   (b) See p. 16 (top).
2. (a) See p. 13, para. 2.
   (b) See p. 20, para. 5.
   (c) See p. 18 (middle).
3. and 4. See p. 13, para. 3.
5. See p. 16.
6. (a) See p. 18, para. 2.
   (b) See p. 20, para. 5.

Chapter 3: The Bible (Pages 23–33)
1. (a), (b) and (c) See p. 23.
2. (a) and (b) See p. 25 (bottom).
3. See p. 26, para. 4.
4. (a) See p. 28.
   (b) See p. 32.
   (c) See p. 29.
5. See p. 24 (bottom).
6. See p. 25, para. 3.
7. See p. 26 (bottom).
8. See p. 23.

KEY TO STUDY SUGGESTIONS

Chapter 4: The History of Theology (Pages 35–45)
1. (a) See p. 36, para. 3.
   (b) and (c) See p. 37.
2. (a) See p. 36 (bottom).
   (b) See p. 42, para. 4.
   (c) See p. 44 (bottom).
3. See p. 35.
4. See p. 36, para. 3.
5. See p. 36.
6. See p. 39.
7. (a), (b) and (c) See p. 43.
   (d) See p. 44.
8. (a), (b) and (c) See p. 44.

Chapter 5: Taking Account of Culture (Pages 47–54)
1. (a) See p. 48. (c) See p. 49.
   (d) See p. 54.
2. (a) See p. 48 (top).
   (b) See p. 50, para. 2.
3. (a) See p. 47, para. 3.
   (b) See p. 48 (middle).
4. See p. 51 (top).
5. See p. 51 (bottom).

Chapter 6: Theologians in Society (Pages 56–66)
1. (a) See p. 56, para. 1.
   (b) See p. 57 (top).
   (c) See p. 57, para. 3.
   (d) and (e) See p. 59 (bottom).
   (f) See p. 61, para. 2.
   (g) See p. 63, para. 4.
2. (a) See p. 60 (top).
   (b) See p. 59, para. 2.
   (c) See p. 65, para. 3.
   (d) See p. 65 (bottom).
3. See p. 60, para. 3.
4. See p. 56.
5. See p. 58, para. 3.
6. See p. 59 (top).
7. (a) and (b) See p. 60.
   (c) and (d) See p. 64.

Chapter 7: The Problem of History (Pages 69–76)
1. (a) See p. 69, para. 2.
   (b) See p. 71, para. 3.
   (c) See p. 72, para. 4.
   (d) See p. 73, para. 4.

KEY TO STUDY SUGGESTIONS

2. See p. 72 (top).
3. (a) See p. 69 (bottom).
   (b) See p. 70 (middle).
   (c) See p. 70 (bottom).
4. (a) and (b) See p. 69.
5. See p. 74.

Chapter 8: Philosophies and Religions (Pages 78–90)
1. See p. 78.
2. (a) p. 78, para. 4.
   (b) See p. 78, para. 2.
   (c) See p. 85 (bottom).
   (d) See p. 81, para. 1.
   (e) See p. 87.
   (f) See p. 84, para. 2.
3. (a) See p. 88, para. 5.
   (b) See p. 89 (bottom).
   (c) See p. 78, para. 3.
   (d) See p. 80, para. 2.
4. See p. 78 (bottom).
5. (a) See p. 80.
   (b) See p. 81, para. 3.
6. See p. 84.
7. See p. 84 (bottom).

Chapter 9: The Challenge of Doing Theology (Pages 92–103)
1. (a) and (b) See p. 98, para. 4.
   (c) See p. 95, para. 2.
   (d) See p. 93, para. 4.
   (e) See p. 100, para. 2.
   (f) See p. 99 (bottom).
2. (a) See p. 101 (top).
   (b) See p. 99 (bottom).
   (c) See p. 100, para. 3.
   (d) See p. 96 (bottom).
   (e) and (f) See p. 97, para. 4.

Index

An asterisk (*) after the page number refers to an entry in the glossary.

Absolute Being, God as 84, 99
Adaptationism 33, 51, 108*
Africa 32, 44–5, 85: culture and theology in 50, 52–3; poverty in 65: *see also* South Africa
Allegories 29
Amos 30
Ancestor worship 52–3
Apocalyptic 29, 108*
Apocrypha 37
Apologetics 10, 96
Apostles' Creed 39
Appasamy, A. J. 54
Aquinas, St Thomas 80
Aramaic 18
ashram 108*
Asia 32, 44, 52, 85; poverty in 65; *see also* India
Athanasian Creed 39
Augsburg Confession 42
Authority
  of the Bible 23–4, 36–7
  of the Church 42–3
Avatars 53–4

Barth, Karl 5, 32, 86, 93–4
Bhagavadgita 109*
Bhakti 54, 109*
Bible 6, 35
  accuracy 31–2, 70–3
  authority 23–4, 36–7
  ideological readings 26–8
  literary 28–31
  systematic theology and 94
  translations 19–20, 31
  understanding 24–6
  see also Gospels; New Testament; Old Testament
Biblical criticism 25–6, 28, 70, 110*

Biblical theology 92, 109*
Black Consciousness 60
Black South African Theology 59–60
Black theology 59, 97, 109*
Boesak, Allan 60, 74
Brahmabandhab Upadhyaya (B. C. Banerji) 84, 89
Buber, Martin 80, 99
Buddhism 85
Bujo, B. 53
Bultmann, R. 16, 71, 80–1
Buthelezi, Manas 60

Calvin, John 26
Canon, formation of 36–7
Capitalism 63, 65
Caste 56, 60–1, 109*
Charismatic movement 41, 108*
Changed perspectives 97
China 20
Christian society 58–9
Christian thought, history of 35–40
Christianity 17–18, 69, 70, 100
  culture and 50, 51
  Greek thought and 78–80
  and non-Christian religions 85–90
Christology 96
Church 10
  authority 42–3
  history 6, 35–42
  and state 58
Church Fathers 36, 38, 79
Class conflict 65
Confessions 42
Conservative theology 2
Context 3, 4, 8, 47, 109*
  of biblical texts 30
  changing 17–20
Contextualization 33, 51–2, 109*

INDEX

Controversies 39
Copernican revolution 87, 110*
Cosmos 84, 99, 110*
Council of Carthage 37
Creeds 3–4, 35, 38–40
    interpretation 40–1
Crucifixion 70, 72
Culture 3, 4, 18, 48–9
    creeds and 40
    theology and 47–54

Dalit theology 60–1
Deism 4, 110*
Demythologists 16
Didache 37
Divine, human and 98–9
Division of labour 57
Docetism 110*
Dogma 6, 38, 45, 110*
Dogmatics 93–8, 110*
Donatism 41–2

Eastern Orthodox Church 4, 40, 115*
Ebeling, 94
Ecclesiology 96
Eclecticism 82, 111*
Economics 57, 59
    theology and 64–6
Election 5, 111*
Empiricism 43
Enlightenment 43, 96, 111*
Epicureans 78, 111*
Epignosis 9
Eschatology 94, 96, 111*
Eschaton 69, 111*
Exclusivism 85–7, 111*
Exegesis 26, 28, 111*
Existentialism 80–1, 98, 111*
Experience
    of God 9–10, 35
    in Greek thought 79
Exploitation 66

Faith 71, 72, 79, 100
    culture and 47–8, 51
    history and 41
    praxis and 102
    see also Statements of faith
Fashole-Luke, E. 52, 53

Feminist theology 27, 61–2, 97
Fundamentalists 8, 23, 24, 112*

General revelation 5, 84
Gnostics 2, 112*
God 2–3, 38–9, 93, 98–9
    existence of 99–100
    in history 73–5
    revelation of, *see* Revelation
    translation of 19–20
Gospels 6, 30, 71
    culture and 51–2
    new contexts for 19–20
Government 57
Greek (language) 18, 31
Greek thought 78–80

Hebrew (language) 31
Hebrews 32, 37
Hegel, G. W. F. 43
Heidegger, Martin 80
Hellenistic Jews 36–7
Heresy 10, 38, 79, 112*
Hermeneutics 26, 28, 100, 112*
Hick, John 87
Hinduism 50, 53, 54, 60, 61, 69–70, 85
    and Christianity 84, 89
Historical method 44
Historical theology 92, 112*
History 29–30, 65
    events in 6, 69, 72–3
    interpretation of 75–6
    linear and cyclical views of 69–70
    as revelation 73–5
Homoousios 112*
Human, and divine 98–9
Humanism 112*
Hume, David 43
Hypostasis 112*

Idealism 80, 112*
Identity, and involvement 102–3
Ideology, Bible and 26–8
Incarnation 53, 54, 69–70
Inclusivism 87–8, 113*
Inculturation 38, 113*
India 60–1
    culture and theology 50, 53–4, 89
    philosophy and theology 84–5

INDEX

Indonesia 62
Injustice 65
Interaction, cultural 49–50
Interpretation 6, 26–8, 40–1, 100–1
Involvement, identity and 102–3

James, Epistle of 32, 37
Jesus Christ 17–18, 71, 72, 79
   in African theology 53
   in Indian theology 54
   saving revelation in 94
JHWH 19
John, Saint 14
Judaism 78
   Palestinian 17, 36–7
Justification 15, 113*

Kant, Immanuel 43, 100
Katoppo, Marianne 62
Kerygma 16, 71
Kibicho, John 89
Kierkegaard, Søren 80, 100
Knowledge 9–10
Korea 64
Kurios (Lord) 18

Language 4
   of the Bible 31
   of the creeds 40–1
   of theology 13–17
Latin America 85
   liberation theology in 64–5, 74–5, 97
Liberation theology 27, 44, 81, 101–2, 113*
   in Latin America 64–5, 74–5, 97
Life-force 84
Linguistic philosophy 14, 113*
Literalists 16, 24
Literary categories 24–6, 28–31
Liturgy 37–8
   indigenous 52
Logical positivism 14, 113*
Logos 78, 79, 87
Luther, Martin 37

Mark, Saint 30
Marx, Karl 65, 81
Materialism 14, 113*
   dialectical 81
Mediating positions 88–100
Metaphor 14–16
Minjung theology 64, 114*
Miracles 70, 72
Missions 51, 86
Mlungu 19
Modimo 19
Moltmann, Jürgen 102
Montanist movement 41
Mosala, Itumeleng 60
Multiculturalism 83, 114*
Mystery cults 18, 114*
Mysticism 93, 114*
Myth 16, 29, 70

Natural theology 5, 96, 114*
Nestorius 40
New Testament 16, 27, 28–9, 32, 37, 69
   interpretation 75
   see also Gospels
Nicene Creed 3, 4, 39, 40
Nkrumah, Kwame 50
Non-Christian religions, Christian theology and 85–90
Non-dualism 84, 111*
Non-Western cultures 49, 50
   Christianity in 19–20
Nyamiti 53
Nyerere, Julius 50, 63

Objective, subjective and 99–101
Oduyoye, Mercy 74
Old Testament 28, 36–7, 69, 86
   historical books 29–30
   interpretation 75
Option for the poor 27, 65
Oral theology 8
Orientalism 83, 114*
Origin of Species, The (Darwin) 43
Orthodoxy 38
   and orthopraxis 101–2
Orthopraxis 38, 65, 74
   and orthodoxy 101–2

Palestinian Christianity 78
Parables 29
Paradoxes 98–102
Patriarchy 27, 97

INDEX

Patristic period 36–42, 115*
Paul, Saint 15, 18, 94
Pentateuch 6, 30
Personal commitment 9, 38, 80
Philosophy 43–4, 78–90
Plato 78, 79
Plotinus 79
Poetry 28–9
Politics 57, 59
   and theology 62–4
Postcolonialism 83, 115*
Postmodernism 81–3, 115*
Poverty 65–6
Praxis 8, 65, 101–2
Preparatio evangelii 88
Prophets 29–30
Protestant Churches 4, 42, 43, 96

Racial discrimination 59–61
Rahner, Karl 87
Reality 2, 100, 101
Reason 7–8, 78
   Enlightenment and 43
Reformation 36, 43, 115*
Reformed Churches 42, 43, 116*
Resurrection 70, 72
Revelation 3, 4–8, 99, 116*
   and non-Christian religions 86, 88, 90
   world history as 73–5
Ritschl, A. 101
Roman Catholic Church 4, 42, 43, 96
Romans, Epistle to 32

Sacramentalists 26, 116*
Sacred history 70
Salvation 15, 75, 90
Sawyerr, Harry 52, 53
Schisms 40
Schleiermacher, F. E. D. 9, 96
Schüssler Fiorenza, Elisabeth 27
Science 1, 43, 116*
Senghor, L. S. 50
Sense data 43, 116*
Septuagint 37, 116*
Setiloane, Gabriel 89
Shepherd of Hermes 37
Social control 57

Social groups 56–7
Society 56–66
Sociology 1, 59
Song, C. S. 74
Soteriology 96, 116*
South Africa, Black theology in 59–60
Special revelation 5
Statements of faith 3–4, 35, 38–40, 42
Stoics 78, 116*
Subjective, objective and 99–101
Supra-empirical reality 2, 13
Symbols 14–16, 29
Systematic theology 92, 93–8, 117*

Technical language 13
Tempels, Placide 84
Tertullian 7
Textual criticism 31
Theological movements 41–2
Theology 2–3
Theos 19
Third World 65–6
   theology 44–5
Thirty-Nine Articles 42
Thlagale, Buti 60
Thomas, M. M. 74
Tillich, Paul 9, 10, 51, 81
Tradition 96, 98
Transcendence 7, 117*
Translation 18, 19–20, 31
Truth 19, 38, 80
Tutu, Desmond 60

Ujamaa 63
Understanding 14, 24–6
Updating 95

Vatican II 42, 117*
Vedanta 84
Virgin birth 72

Wealth 57
Westminster Confession 42
Wiles, Maurice 97
Women 61–2
Word of God 99
   Bible as 24, 71

www.ingramcontent.com/pod-product-compliance
Lightning Source LLC
Chambersburg PA
CBHW071211070526
44584CB00019B/2990